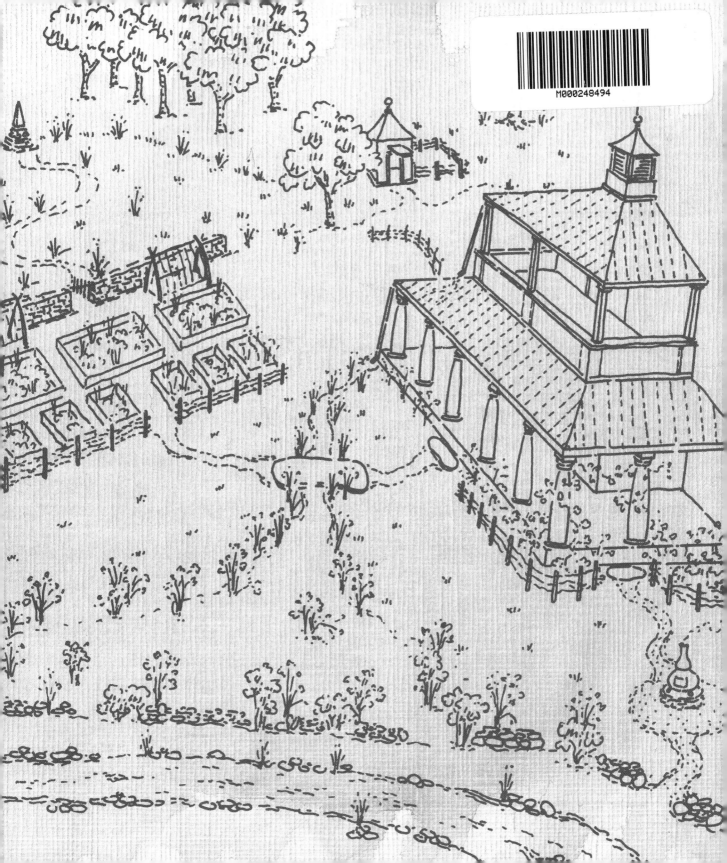

Into the
WEEDS

Into the WEEDS

by Tama Matsuoka Wong

Photographs by
Ngoc Minh Ngo

illustrations by
BOBBI ANGELL
AND WIL WONG

Hardie Grant
NORTH AMERICA

TABLE OF CONTENTS

Introduction 8

CHAPTER ONE
A CASE FOR
WILD GARDENS 12

CHAPTER TWO
FINDING VALUE
ON THE LAND 22

CHAPTER THREE
CONNECTING SPACES 44

CHAPTER FOUR
KNOWING PLANTS 62

CHAPTER FIVE
TIME AND CHANGE 96

CHAPTER SIX
GARDEN BEDS 110

CHAPTER SEVEN
STEWARDSHIP 140

CHAPTER EIGHT
MAKING MORE PLANTS 160

CHAPTER NINE
PRESERVING BOUNTY 184

CHAPTER TEN
CREATING MEMORIES 202

CHAPTER ELEVEN
THE FUTURE IS UNKNOWN 224

Epilogue 230

Acknowledgments 232

Index 233

PROJECTS, ACTIVITIES, RECIPES, TOP FORAGING PLANTS

PROJECTS *P*

28 Chicken Wire Cages

30 Enclosing a Wild(ish) Patch

36 Woven Wattle Edging

38 Open-Lashed Edging

58 Wild Wood Gate

60 Attaching a Gate to a Post

120 Compost Bin Center

128 Fencing for Garden Beds

132 A-Frame Trellis

138 Porch Vine Garland

156 Deer Fence

216 Chicken Wire Flower Frog

218 Wildflower Leis

223 Juniper Firestarters

ACTIVITIES *A*

54 How to Make a Path

66 Dandelion Leaf Study

102 How To: Meadow Doctoring

166 Collecting Wild Seeds in the Field

175 Trench Planting

180 Grow Lights

190 Prepare Leafy Greens for Freezing

212 Using Wild Plants in Arrangements

222 Smudge Sticks

RECIPES *R*

79 Clammy Goosefoot Forager's Salad Dressing

155 Japanese Knotweed Pickle and Soda

170 Lemon Basil and Wild Lemon Balm Pesto

178 Longevity Spinach

179 Lime Leaf, Galangal, and Lemongrass Meatballs

191 Sour Cherry and Wild Berry Jam

192 Spruce Tip Mocktail

194 Fig Leaf Gimlet

196 Mulberry Shrub

199 Feral Apple Spread

206 Honeysuckle Tea

TOP FORAGING PLANTS TO SAVOR

77 Lambsquarters

81 Purslane

82 Dandelion

84 Wild Broccoli Rabe and Mustards

86 Wood Sorrels

87 Chickweed

88 Wild Chives

90 Galinsoga

91 Nettle

93 Sumac

95 Juniper

Introduction

"We are stardust, we are golden,
 and we've got to get ourselves back to the garden. . ."

—JONI MITCHELL

My mother was home, at my house, when she passed away. She died peacefully, a last wisp of breath, and as I flung the doors open to the garden, the late autumn breezes wafted in, caressing her face, carrying her last wishes out to the meadow and over the trees into the sky.

We had been advised by the local hospice team to call them immediately, as they would need to come over and record the time of death. They would alert funeral services; everything had been set up and ready to take my mother away. But in that moment, I didn't want to interrupt her passage. Her body was still warm, the breeze still gentle. I didn't want other people to handle her, just yet. I wished for her spirit to be set free from the body that could no longer hold her, so that she could roam and dance over the garden, as she longed to do.

Buddhists say not to move the body for at least five hours after death because it is a time of passage. I felt the same after giving birth, as my daughter lay on my chest for an hour or more, snuggling, snuffling, mother and child. Not whisked off for weighing and measuring, inserting eye drops.

So I told them not to come for five hours. They said they respected my "religion," but it would mean, they said, that the time of death, which could not be recorded by me, would be five hours later. I accepted this as the strange way of the modern world.

It was also the rule, according to state regulations, that we could not attend her cremation but that we could choose what would go with her.

I knew immediately what my mother would wish for: a simple pine box, and plants in line with that season.

I told the funeral director we didn't need any flowers that had been gathered by strangers and held in warehouses. They would seem fleshy and gaudy atop the simple pine. Instead, I gathered plants from the meadow garden for my mother. She loved purple, and there were still some asters and ironweed wildflowers, their long-stemmed faces pointing upward to the sky. There were some spent Queen Anne's lace and mountain mint, ivory and brown, finished with their season of flowering but still beautiful structurally. And there were aromatics for the fire: juniper berries and cedarwood.

These ceremonial gifts from the garden would accompany her where we could not.

A forager's bouquet.

How could I have known what it would become when I first had an itch for a garden like the one I remembered from my childhood summers, mucking about outdoors with my mother? Her eyes sparkled when she taught me "there is nothing like the feel of the earth in your hands." I loved the unstructured rhythm of those almost-idle summer days when we might set out in the morning to dig a row but end up making a campion bouquet. The one task we set to in earnest was plucking what grew from that earth, whether planted by us or sprouting wild from the soil—dandelion shoots, wild mulberries, spring pea shoots, and wild chives—bringing them to the back porch and inside to the kitchen fragrant with the aroma of good things cooking.

I also had vague visions of gardens of older times: the Hanging Gardens of Babylon, the Great Plains of the buffalo, those vast gardens tended by the Comanche, the Crow, the Apache, the steppes of the Mongols, and more ancient secrets yet: the stewards of the wild spaces when there was only wild and not agriculture. The gardens of the gatherers.

People who have settled for more than a generation on a terrain have passed down their memories of the movements and the grooves in the earth, its seasons to gather and to grow, and to celebrate the plants and wildlife. These natural lands did not lie untouched by human hands, but rather were tended by humans, who were and are a part of the Wild.

When I turned eighteen, I moved away from my mother's wild gardens in New Jersey. I spent much of the next thirty years working and traveling in densely populated cities: Tokyo, Shanghai, Mumbai, Hong Kong, London, New York City. There was no earth on the streets to tend to and, come spring in Hong Kong, longing for the wilderlands, I would escape with friends and coworkers on weekends to hike the open steep hills. Not twenty minutes from the high-rise buildings, the Dragons Back trail was lined with blooms of blush-pink crepe myrtle and orange lantana lanterns, the winding path dropping steeply on either side down to the South China Sea. These rambles meant freedom from urban confinement, from a cubicled world seen through the filter of blue-light screens—a space and time to burst out and breathe, to discover.

Hiking for me was not about exercise and fitness. I lagged behind, lost, intent on the ground, or the changing maritime clouds, filled with random walking thoughts: "Ah, so this is what subtropical means" (in Hong Kong you find both temperate species as well as tropical); "Are these wild plants or escaped from cultivated gardens?" (both wild and cultivated and "crossovers"); and, most curiously, "Oy, this is the same weedy plant I saw in New Jersey in the driveway, in a crack in the sidewalk in Florida, and in Japan." These plants I could recognize almost all over the temperate world—some indigenous, some naturalized, mostly overlooked or even actively derided, the ones that people decided were not worthy, and certainly not part of their plans.

Or, in other words, what people call "weeds."

Decades later, I moved back to New Jersey, forty minutes from my childhood home. I wanted to go back to my mother's garden. I finally owned land—twenty-eight acres that were not being used for anything in particular—and two old houses that needed fixing up, and had a family who simply couldn't believe the amount of open space in America.

Returning to the United States was a rediscovery. I remembered very little about specific plants or their names. I didn't pay attention enough to learn them at the time because I thought I could always just lazily ask my mother, a walking plant encyclopedia. Also, I knew nothing about what to do with fallow land, just that I appreciated it like never before now that I had traversed the world. Whereas before I looked at a New Jersey yard as just something to walk across, I now saw it as a place to immerse my family, a place uncommonly large and precious. And I didn't want to spoil it.

Bordering our land on the southernly edge was a creek which was a Category One waterway in New Jersey. I was worried about fresh water, having read headlines about chemical waste and sewage dumped in waterways. I didn't want polluted water to flow by and even flood our land. What lay upstream and downstream? The New Jersey Conservation Foundation contacted landowners about the importance of this creek and sought to protect and preserve the watershed for future generations.

I asked them about the pond in the back. Was the water quality okay? Could we swim in it? Was it choking with algae or was that duckweed? The New Jersey Conservation folks told Leslie Sauer Jones, neighbor, naturalist, and founder of the landscape architecture firm Andropogon, about my questions and she decided to stop by for a walkaround: Leslie, towering over us, had an unquenchable passion for telling stories, in her low, raspy voice, of the woods and their plants. She was like a pied piper; my daughters and I trailed irresistibly behind her as she pointed out that some places were special remnants of a precolonial settlement age whereas other spots, choked with invasive plants, needed to be kept under the thumb of control, and by the way, did I know I had the makings of an exquisite wet meadow rolling down toward the pond?

All land, be it a formal hardscaped botanical garden, farmland, a sprawling backyard, community garden, or public park, office courtyard, abandoned lot, even a windowsill pot... Any of these can shelter a little wilderness, a piece of paradise. So, how to find it and steward it—or at least not spoil its treasures? Much of the earth has been despoiled, degraded, paved over, dumped on, bulldozed over by the rush of modernity. Wilderness exists in increasingly smaller parcels, crisscrossed by asphalt, concrete, and steel. Even where no people live, we extract the natural resources, and where we farm or pave over, we create barrenness or monocultures of crop commodities.

To rewild and reconnect, however, does not mean to do nothing, to leave land untouchable. It means we need to rethink the way we garden, and rethink our own role, as stewards and managers of the land. The goal is not to create a garden, to make and then be finished. Instead, the goal is TO garden, the act of gardening, with intention: with intention of observation, and intention of pace, every week its own series of ephemeral moments. For, in caring for a garden, we bring nature next to us, hold it within our hands, embrace curiosity and humbleness, and in doing so glimpse some of the secrets of the universe.

My hope is that, if there is anything to take away from this book, even if you never touch a drill to build raised beds, or transplant any seedlings, you might begin to look differently at the land and the plants that grow there. And maybe throw off some assumptions about what chores must be tended to, and adjust to a less-structured time frame and rhythm, placing greater trust in your own observations. You may start to value what is already there. Once you discover the natural footprints of your land, you mark these places, wind down some paths. Over time you might even edit and tweak, developing a mutual relationship of stewardship and productivity: you forage and harvest and also nurture and seed. You celebrate and mourn through the gifts of the land. This is the Forager's Garden, and it celebrates the land and our connection to it in a deep, intrinsic way.

CHAPTER ONE

A CASE *for* WILD GARDENS

WILD GARDENS OF THE MIDDLE GROUND 17

THE WILD IS NOT A BLANK SLATE 19

DESIGN ELEMENTS OF A WILD GARDEN 20

WHAT DOES IT MEAN to garden the wild, and where is the elusive Wild? I can never seem to explain what it is that I really do. Foraging, full-time, isn't listed as a job in the census categories. But I know what people think I do. Every spring, my phone beeps: chefs, students, families, urban gardeners, the merely curious…hankering to escape and get out into the wild. "Take me out with you," they enjoin, to enjoy the season, to pick free things and unearth hidden secrets of nature. They expect a lot: a hunt, though nothing too strenuous, and other times just gathering the bounty of nature. Spring fever dreams.

So, I sense a slight deflation when I take people round to the back of my old shed, point out a fallow ditch where nettle is growing, or spend an hour or more squatting, cutting quickweed or purslane in between the rows of my vegetable garden. "Tama, this is not the Wild."

What they are hoping for is something more remote. Sometimes I give in, and I can hear their excitement when I invite them to go foraging in kayaks in the Pine Barrens. After all, the Barrens are stunning. Hard to imagine that only a little more than an hour from the concrete metropolis lies one of the largest wild preserves in the eastern United States outside of the Everglades. Not only is this place unknown, but its fine sands, the consistency of sugar, veil an underground aquifer of some of the purest water on the continent. In a kayak, you can splice through white lily pads floating in an endless stream; an egret and wild ducks rise from deep cool waters. Their calls trail away into the stillness. To get there, you'll drive along dusty sand trails through disused cranberry fields overgrown with bracken and clethra. Strange little plants are scattered in the open sands: carnivorous sundews and bear grass; pine frogs croak from the trees.

And when the breeze kicks up over the open moors, the whisper of pine and salt spray wafts across the coastal plains from the ocean a few miles away. It's a magical conjured world.

And there's good foraging, too. The best wild highbush blueberries grow on the edge, along the banks of the bogs, their roots tapping into the clear cool water, the branches laden and full, asking to be plucked. Everyone starts grabbing berries… "Wait a minute! I always check for quality control!" Smiles freeze, as if expecting some quality-control inspector to emerge from behind a pine tree. I explain, patiently, that every wild berry bush tastes a little different, so you need to sample each bush to see how delicious it is. Everyone loves this kind of quality control and starts sampling. My colleague Larry goes for the super-overripe wrinkly ones because their flavor is so concentrated, almost like a blueberry Starburst. Chris, my neighbor, prefers to throw an entire handful of various berries in his mouth so he gets the blend of flavors; each bush, each cluster, shades of difference. This is the flavor of the wild. And of course, it's as it should be, a mirror of the diversity of nature, a symphony of notes and harmonies. But you can also find flavors of the wild closer to home.

When I begin a foraging "tour" I tell people to look right around them, even off to the side of the parking lot. The tour organizers may pull me aside and in low tones tell me that they hoped this hike would be an adventure deep into the forest, where the wild things live. People don't think that something growing by the side of a house is the wild, but top foraging spots are often found right around where people live (caveat: avoid overly sprayed, asphalted, or polluted environments). Weeds evolve to take advantage of conditions created by human intervention. Weedy plants have accompanied humans or been stowed away as cargo from places where they are relished; they then thrive on new grounds that are often open, maybe scratched up or worked on. When I look around the ordinary places right around me, I see an inviting buffet. These are the fallow areas, cracks between stones, the out-of-season raised beds, the sides of house foundations and doorways, the vacant lots. These are the places that are open to wild things.

The second-best foraging areas I find are in the "in between" areas; the areas that cross over between the forest and field, or forest and farm, along brackish waters where salty meets fresh. Ecologists and ethnobotanists call this the edge. In Europe they call it the hedgerow, in Japan the *satoyama*. These areas have always been prized for their richness and diversity. Many Native Americans spent more time on open floodplains and forest edges than they did in the middle of closed canopy forests. When I walk along an edge, on one side a sunlit field and on the other a half-dappled opening to a forest or a line of shrubs, there are many small herbs growing underfoot, sheltered by the edge.

So, instead of creating boundaries between wild and not wild, I like letting plants merge next to each other. I don't need to impose hard lines demarking my garden, whether by hardscape, mulching, plastic weed control, or chemical eradication, for in the end nature slips through the boundaries and blurs them. And this mixing is something beautiful.

What about the compost pile outside my kitchen—is that wild? For many years, I have foraged pawpaws in October, when their skin is still green and their flesh yields slightly to the touch. I always freeze some golden, creamy purée, and toss the peels and seeds around the back of the stone shed with the compost. A couple years ago, I was poking around that side of the shed, when I was irritatingly slapped in the face with some leaves. My first thought was, "What is a bloody tree doing in my compost pile?" My second thought was that there was something super familiar about this leaf, twelve inches long, oar shaped... But it was the smell that got me: a heady, burnt, tropical sort of scent. Nothing else smells quite like a pawpaw leaf. And once it had hit me—literally—I realized I was standing in the middle of a mini-grove of little pawpaw trees. The trees were growing up spindly, only eight inches apart; I waited to see which ones bore fruit and then thinned out the smaller nonfruiting suckers.

Is this patch "cultivated" because I had a hand in their propagation? I did little more than the raccoon who also pilfered discarded pawpaws from the same compost pile and slunk away to enjoy the fruits some twenty yards away. I discovered these raccoon-planted pawpaw patches, too, and it seems foolhardy to clear them. Of all the hundreds of pounds of seeds scattered here and there from my annual pawpaw forages, it was on these spots that they germinated. Some confluence of conditions, genetics, soil, and half shelter has blessed these patches with pawpaws. So, I let the plants grow where they may. And I moved the compost pile.

Can I take credit for this exuberant patch? Not really. I had a hand in its spread and practiced a bit of tending. But mostly it was benign neglect, a far cry from the linear rows of pawpaw trees set in mulch I have seen on some farms. In nature, pawpaws don't grow in rows. They grow like my compost pile saplings.

So, what is truly wild? When did we leave the wild behind and start cultivating? The answer is that we never did and despite our best efforts, we've never really extinguished the ways of the wild.

WILD GARDENS OF THE MIDDLE GROUND

It has long been accepted that hunter-gatherers were the starting point in the race from nomadic life to modern agriculture. European explorers who first came to the North American continent noted that here was a wild land so fertile that the peoples that lived there did not need to farm. They could see no orchards with neat rows. No tilled fields. What they perceived were hunter-gatherers whose lives involved roaming and hunting from wild place to wild place. They did not "own" or farm any particular site.

Of course, this thinking has changed. Peoples in North America and beyond did hunt and gather, but their gathering included tending: planting, seeding, culling, and some patch burning to clear the way for preferred plants. And this era of shepherding wild gardens was not just a blip on the way to better progress. Anthropologists call these practices—part foraging and part farming or gardening—the Middle Ground (Bruce Smith, "Low-Level Food Production," *Journal of Archaeological Research,* March 2001).

This Middle Ground is not specific to any particular people, or any particular place. Nor is it over. Still today, in parts of Asia, Africa, Central and South America, Europe, and rural patches of the United States, people are working with plant communities in the way of the Middle Ground, as many did in the Jōmon period in Japan or the Natufian period in the Levant (the land bridge between Africa and East Asia). We are only beginning to scratch the surface of the field practices of our human ancestors. It could even be said that it is industrial agriculture that is the anomaly, practiced only for a couple of decades and suitable only for certain extensive flatlands, requiring large capital investment and annual credit financing, whereas the Middle Ground is standard for much of the world's population. These ways persist because they make common sense: because most of the planet forms pockets, not expanses, of arable land, and because this way of living taps deep into the primordial relationship between the people, the plants, and the land.

And what are these common-sense ways? Anthropologists and ethnobotanists have categorized Middle Ground methods, which they call "in situ" management, to include:

1. **Systematic gathering.** It's just common sense that if something is in season, you get a lot of it. Focus on the species in peak season, when they are nutrient dense.

2. **Let standing,** also sometimes known as the practice of "sparing" or "tolerating." Whaddaya know! I've been practicing this method all my life. I laughed out loud when I read this in a scholarly journal; I LOVE this category. Leave preferred annuals standing, making sure that the

surrounding ground is open enough that there will be good seed-to-soil contact. (See page 163.)

3. **Encouraging growing.** Burning and taming of vegetation to favor particular plant species, sowing seeds, planting cuttings, or buds. It makes sense to encourage weedy but useful plants to grow in between rows or under crops. In Mexico, corn is a common crop, but so are lambsquarters (*Chenopodium* spp.), one of many traditional wild herbs called quelites. Favored quelites are now propagated by scattering the seeds in between primary crops.

4. **Protection.** Peoples deliberately eliminated competitors and predators by editing out less-favored competitor plants, pruning back trees or underbrush for easier access and greater fruit-bearing, and to protect favored plants from frost.

THE WILD IS NOT
A BLANK SLATE

I consider myself a practitioner of the Middle Ground, a forager-farmer. Although I started off aspiring to garden in the ways of photos in books and magazines, those ways didn't work out for me. Once I planted a small rosebush I bought from a nursery. It felt like the moment I turned my back the bush was surrounded by weeds. I soon discovered that unless I had time every day of the week to control them, by the weekend these unwanted plants had overtaken the struggling rosebush. I would wake up Saturday morning and gnash my teeth when I looked outside, and no matter how I toiled, by the end of the day I ended up feeling stressed about how I could never catch up and was always falling behind on trying to make a proper garden.

That's when I started thinking differently. Once I threw off my thoughts about negligence and control, I began to appreciate what I had been missing. I realized that the wild and weedy plants had a certain charm. I had never looked closely at them, but in the light of dawn or at dusk their colors glowed like torches. It was not only how they looked, but how they smelled, felt in the fingertips, what happened when I cut them. I also started to craft small things from these wild woody plants' cast-off twigs and twining vines. I noticed how the branches grew, the texture of their bark, the layers of soft inner wood. The frustrating strength of a twining woody vine became a tensile support for a wire fence or other structure.

My expectations now move with the rhythms of the season, and I can better savor the present moment. I appreciate the time and conditions it took for an oak tree to grow and thrive. And I don't overlook a wild grove of spicebush that may have grown up despite predators and pests for decades. Or a patch of spring ephemeral herbs, perennial but visible for only a few short weeks a year. All these are part of the heritage of the land and are not quickly reproduced.

Now, instead of feeling like a failed gardener, I feel alive and rejuvenated. I have learned to appreciate what I have and to live in that exact moment.

DESIGN ELEMENTS OF A WILD GARDEN

I'm keen to enjoy all the land has to offer. I garden with the wild, without judging bad versus good, and with my eyes attuned to reading the land. The land is not a blank slate. There are high and low spots, there are natural areas of shelter from the wind, there are wetter places and drier places. Moving through the land, I see that it is full of the wildness of living things: patches of ephemerals, vernal pools where the rare salamanders come out en masse to spawn on misty spring nights. These elements do not appear on a map or in a landscaper's design. They are elements of the field.

Light: Natural light, that is; wild, unfiltered light from the sun, which governs our waking energy, restful sleep, and of course vitamin D with its many health benefits. Sleep and wakefulness are tethered together by light. As Andrew Huberman, a Stanford School of Medicine neurobiology professor, advises: try to get light from the sun, outdoors, not through a window, within ninety minutes of waking. Between two and ten minutes if a sunny day, twenty minutes if the day is cloudy or stormy. The light to the eyes, to the brain, triggers waking, and the morning colors of light are distinguished by the brain and body from sunset light. Foraging, or gardening, in my outdoor office gets me away from squinting through artificial light. May I suggest spending five minutes in the morning outside with light, instead of an extra scroll on the phone or looking at social media? As

you do this, start to watch where the sun rises and sets around you. How do the colors and shadows change the garden as the day passes? The colors of the sky are part of the wildness in every garden. In fifteen minutes, the light will change. You can find the points north and south on a map. But to connect the points to the field, you need how to understand how it feels by orienting with the sun.

Air: Take a breath of the loamy air in the forest, the cedar scents, or the breezes of the open fields. Are they gentle or strong gales? Where and in which direction do they blow? When we sit on the porch at the end of a long summer day, a cool breeze kicks up from the forest on the ridge down to the creek, its trail refreshing us.

Soil: What makes up the soil? Minerals, dead matter, living matter, gas, water... soil also includes rocks, roots, debris, bugs, crawlers. Soils can be old or new, and the texture of the soil may tend more toward sandy or loamy or claylike; the mineral content may be alkaline or acidic. Grab a handful of soil and examine it closely. Some urban visitors to my garden don't want to touch the soil; they think that soil is dirt, as in dirty. But soils are the primary provider of nutrients for plants on earth. Soils are part of the permanent cycle of germination, growth, decay, and decomposition, and they are intrinsically connected to water. Before making any judgments about good dirt or bad dirt, poor soils or rich soils, think about what your goals are. Some fine wild native plants thrive in soil considered too "poor" for agriculture. You don't need to get a soil test to enjoy nature, of course. And there are online resources that can give you a general framework for understanding the soils of your area of interest.

Flora: Go outdoors and look at your feet. What plants do you see? No matter how tiny, how meager looking, plants that can grow out of a crack in the foundation, in a fallow bed, belie an inner resiliency. These plants can be single specimens or patches growing wild without human design. How do the plants grow, where do they live? Start with just one or two plants, but begin to watch them intently through the days and nights. Dandelion flowers will only bloom in full sun; on a cloudy day, at night, or in the refrigerator they close up like a trap and refuse to be pried open. The plants found on a site can tell you the story of the land. A patch of earth is unique just as every person is unique—every place has its own DNA. It is hard to overstate the specialness of native plants that grow on my patch of land. They have genetically adapted over perhaps many hundreds of years to my region and represent a biodiversity and resilience that cannot be replicated by transporting plants in. Plants grow in communities and so a hodgepodge of transplants will more resemble a museum of propped-up plants than a natural, thriving ecosystem.

Water: Without water there can be no garden. Where is the local watershed, the local creek or river that your land belongs to; where does the water run off? Where does the wild water—not irrigated water—naturally settle into the ground? A wild garden and its plants use water opportunistically, taking advantage of its natural highs and lows. You can tell where the land is more wet by identifying which plants grow there. If you find common rush (*Juncus effusus*) there is a 99 percent chance you are standing in a wetland.

These elements make up the wild; just go outside, take notice, even if you first think that there is nothing around you, that what is there is ugly or not desirable. I began as a failed gardener: everything I planted died, my garden was unkempt and scraggly. But I learned to appreciate the elements and found that almost everything that I was looking for was already here the whole time.

CHAPTER TWO

FINDING VALUE *on* THE LAND

ELEMENTS OF A PLACE 35

MARKING SPOTS 27

Ⓟ   Chicken Wire Cages 28

Ⓟ   Enclosing a Wild(ish) Patch 30

MAKING AN EDGE WITH WILD WOOD 34

Ⓟ   Woven Wattle Edging 36

Ⓟ   Open-Lashed Edging 38

SIGNS AND LABELS 42

ELEMENTS
OF A PLACE

Once the bones of the land and its elements take shape, take note of plants, views, objects, things that mean something to you; it could be just a spot to linger around. There may be a few "spokesplants" that would be a shame to lose. These spots and specimens are worthy and represent the heritage of the land. Here are some from my home:

- **A mayapple patch under the trees.** In spring, under dappled light, my daughters squealed delightedly when I told them these were fairy umbrellas. A naturalist neighbor pointed out that the colony was far older than the oak tree they were growing under. A mayapple seed will not generally form a rhizome for at least five years and may not bloom for twelve years. Colonies grow mainly underground at an average rate of five inches a year, so a large colony like this one may well be over one hundred years old. The entire plant is toxic except for the fruit, but even that I leave, as it's a favorite treat of the eastern box turtle. I appreciate these and other small ephemerals of the spring and watch my patches with fervor.

- **A puddle or depression, wet only in the spring.** Many people curse the wet areas. The lawn won't grow there. Can't mow or drive anything without getting stuck in the spring mud. Instead of cursing them, hang up a proud sign announcing "Vernal Pond" or "Frog Mating Puddle." Vernal ponds are wet in spring but dry up in the summer. Since they are very shallow, they provide spawning areas, food, shelter, and habitat for amphibians including uncommon turtles and salamanders.

- **A beech tree stand.** Although the beech tree, *Fagus grandifolia*, is not uncommon, finding several of them growing together, with their smooth, elephant-gray bark, is a striking sight. I found only a few mature trees high on the ridge. I call them the Three Brothers. Mature beeches cast a dense shade so there are no weeds underneath except the fascinating beechdrops and Indian pipes—a ghostly pale parasitic plant that grows around beeches and is not found anywhere else on my land. I refuse to disturb the soil around the beech tree roots, because they are shallow and sensitive to injury. Beeches can sprout stump suckers where a tree has blown down, or root suckers that can form low thickets. If the mature tree dies, these will shoot up in its place.

- **Common witch hazel (*Hamamelis virginiana*).** I found a grove of this growing on the ridge in my woods. A botanist friend told me not to believe the designation "common"; some plants that used to be common are now declining or hardly to be found, as is the case with witch hazel. Perhaps one of the reasons is because they are a magnet for Japanese honeysuckle, an invasive vine. Honeysuckle had grown and wrapped tightly around the small trunks of the witch hazel in my woods, and over time, as the tree tried to grow, the honeysuckle cut deeper and deeper into the trunk. I cut the honeysuckle vine at the base where it sprung from the earth and untwined it where it was strangling the trees.

- **Swamp goldenrod (*Solidago patula*).** I only noticed this unusual goldenrod, also known as round-leafed goldenrod, because the leaves were wider than a ladle, so different from the widespread Canada goldenrod with its skinnier leaves. There were two of them growing in a wet spot on the way to the pond. A field botanist friend identified it as swamp goldenrod. I marked this area so that it would not be mowed and, as the years have become wetter and wetter, hundreds of swamp goldenrod now march in line along the muddy spring path, and indeed I find it spreading to the driveway and my garden beds.

- **Old-fashioned trees and shrubs.** A crabapple, a scraggly lilac bush that some long-ago owners planted... I don't mark them, but I appreciate their blooms and the knowledge that they have persisted for at least sixty years, a gift from the past, so I use the flowers as well as the fruits.

These are not problem areas. Their very unusualness makes them destinations, and creating markers ensures they won't be easily forgotten.

MARKING SPOTS:
Logs, Stones, Driveway Poles, and Chicken Wire

Found rocks make great marker materials. Stone is permanent: it's heavy and carries gravitas, physically and spiritually. Wild stone is asymmetric, rough-hewn, with shades of ocher, charcoal, eggplant, and thin mica. Stone is also cultural, an ancient way of marking permanent memorials. Stacked stones can represent a respect for the East and a form of prayer as in the cairns of Scotland or the *ishidōrō* (stone lanterns) of Japan.

Rock collecting is not permitted in many public and national parks. Rocks may at times be sourced from masons, construction contractors, farmers, or excavators. A mason told me that he often finds iconic old rocks where there is a bridge or other teardown.

A fallen log or a standing dead tree can provide rich organic nutrients and shelter for a host of animals, birds, insects, and seedlings as well as fungi. Instead of hiring a contractor to haul away or chip up the wood, you can mark these trees in the Japanese Shinto tradition of respect by wrapping them with rope, or hanging cord with raffia tassels or white paper streamers from them.

Orange reflective driveway poles can serve as quick placeholders. They are inexpensive and lightweight, but sturdy and very easy to spot. When I see something with potential, it's time to jab a stick into the ground. Realizing that a driveway marker does not keep away avid mowers or deer, I'll follow up with something more substantial, either chicken wire (see page 28) or stone.

Chicken wire is an excellent material to have on hand. It can be reshaped and reused year after year and used in fencing, supports, and in ikebana as flower frogs. It can also be placed at the bottom of beds to protect them from tunneling voles or woodchucks.

Chicken Wire Cages

I discovered an unusual shrublike plant growing on a corner curve where mowed grass met meadow. I hadn't planted any shrub there but could tell it was a sapling. I jabbed a driveway marker on the spot and then returned on the weekend with a small chicken wire cage to protect the plant at least until I could identify it. I took a photo and shopped it around to the small cadre of friends and colleagues that can't think of anything they would rather do than solve a puzzle of "what is this plant?" It turned out the plants were wild persimmon saplings. The cage protected them from random deer that entered when a tree fell on the fencing as well as overzealous mowers, and they grew several feet. Based on this success I now have cages dotted around, marking various spots, to protect small sumac trees and spicebush saplings as well as to surround a nascent nettle patch. · **This project will yield one cage, 48 inches / 1.2 m high and about 36 inches / 91.44 cm square interior area.**

Chicken wire is a metal mesh of galvanized (rust-proof) steel that is commonly sold in rolls. The standard gauge thickness of the wire is 20. A heavier gauge such as 19 will make the fence stronger but also more difficult to cut through and form. Some "flimsiness" also helps deter woodchucks who may find it difficult to climb over. The hexagonal gaps are about 1 inch / 2.54 cm wide, but you can opt for smaller if concerned with small voles. You can lay this mesh on the bottom of your garden bed to prevent them from digging up under the bed.

Feel free to purchase a **standard roll**, which contains 300 inches / 7.62 m of chicken wire, and use it for other projects like the Chicken Wire Flower Frog on page 216. Standard gauge is 20.

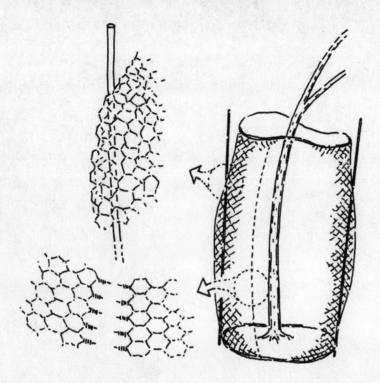

MATERIALS

1 length of 1-inch / 2.54 cm mesh hexagonal chicken wire, 48 inches / 1.21 m high by 75 inches / 1.9 m long

Wire cutters

2 narrow straight sticks or driveway markers, minimum height 48 inches / 1.21 m

Hammer or mallet

METHOD

1. Partially unroll the mesh on a flat surface.

2. Measure and cut a length about 75 inches / 1.9 m long. Make the cut in the middle of each wire cell so that the wire ends are open.

3. Bring one side up to meet the other, overlapping the ends by 1–2 inches / 2.54–5.08 cm, and bend the open wire ends back over the other ends along the length of the cage, twisting if necessary to secure it.

4. Tip upright and place over the plant you wish to protect.

5. Thread one stick through one cell at the top of the wire and then through another cell toward the bottom of the wire.

6. Repeat with the other stick on the opposite end of the cage.

7. Use the hammer or mallet to push the sticks at least 3 inches / 7.62 cm into the ground.

Enclosing a Wild(ish) Patch

Take advantage of a certain "weedy" patch that is already ripe for opportunity or a fallow area that is hard to "maintain." Some wild or semi-wild things already grow there: dandelions, chickweed, or even common milkweed. My friend who lives in a suburb told me she wanted a wildish area, but her husband doesn't like things that look unkempt, so she was nervous about having an area that looked "out of control." She settled on an area about fifteen square feet, tucked off to the side of the main yard. A portion of an existing vegetable raised bed or other ornamental garden bed would also easily work.

Starting small allows for adjustments. At this early stage the plot has every potential—or maybe no potential—so you don't want to create something too permanent until you see how things shape up. I usually test things out first because plants will thrive where they want to be, with a little bit of nudging.

It's a good idea to mark off the area because, if you are like me, one or more of the following may happen:

- Over the winter, I forget where it is and it ends up permanently lost.

- Unless I am always on weed patrol, other family members may trample all over it, or friends may take their dog for a walk through it.

- Whoever is doing the mowing or weed whacking cuts it down so that it is uniform with the surrounding area.

I try to mark off sections that have a cluster of interesting plants that I want more of: yarrow, wild spearmint, wild ginger. Mark off the chosen area with any visible barrier, like fallen branches, vines, bushes, even small tree trunks. I use young pitch pine and juniper saplings and branches to mark off an outline and create a barrier for this area. When things start happening in the patch, I go one step further and create a sturdier enclosure as a boundary. I make these with materials I have on hand, and they can be as neat or messy as you like. I move the posts of the enclosure easily to reconfigure the shape or increase or decrease the area depending on how the "test" patch is growing. · **This project will yield one enclosure for a 9-foot / 2.74 m long by 11-foot / 3.35 m wide patch.**

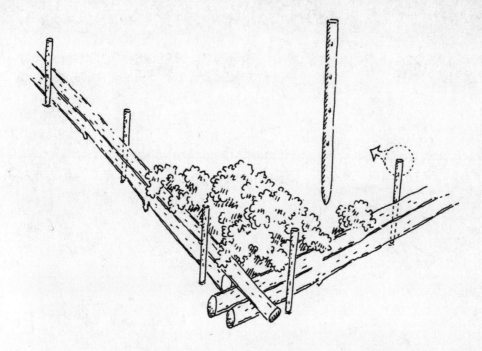

For the length: 2–4 branches or sapling trunks, 9 feet / 2.74 m long and at least 2 inches / 5.08 cm diameter

For the width: 2–4 branches or sapling trunks, 11 feet / 3.35 m long and at least 2 inches / 5.08 cm diameter

24 steel rebar pins, 18 inches / 45.72 cm long and ¾ inch / 1.9 cm diameter, with pointed ends

Hammer or mallet

METHOD

1. Lay four of the sapling trunks (two of each length) on the ground in a rectangular shape.

2. Position six pins diagonally opposite each other so there are three pins on each side of the first trunk, driving them into the ground with a mallet so that they hug the trunk in place. Leave approximately 24 inches / 60.96 cm between pins. If a pin hits a rock or root, move the pin a little to the left or right. This method is extremely forgiving. Repeat with the remaining pins on the other three trunks.

3. Stack the second four saplings on top of the lower set of trunks, adjusting the pins if necessary to hold the stack in place and so that the saplings do not roll out.

4. Start with a minimum of two sapling trunks stacked on each side and then continue to stack over time or as you find more woody material.

MAKING AN EDGE WITH WILD WOOD

How would anyone guess that in the weeds under the Japanese plum tree grows some sweet woodruff I am saving for a chef, or that the patch of wild yarrow in the grass is not for mowing down? The wild mint and oregano area that somehow spread out from leftover summer barbecue debris tends to get quite feisty in the summer. I keep it from flopping all over onto the path by marking an "edge" there. Outlining these spaces with natural materials can look beautiful and give a tiny bit of structure to a wild and sprawly garden, especially in the height of the season, when things are growing like weeds.

The place you tend does not have to belong to you. It may be the side of a community garden, church grounds, a YMCA or community center, a berm around a retention basin, a vacant lot, a rooftop or balcony, or the back side of a shopping center. Obtain clear permission to forage and check that the property owner does not spray herbicide or other toxins. Mark your permitted area. See what grows there. Remember that permission to forage still means you are a guest and that your host is trusting you to leave no footprint.

I make two types of edging: woven wattle edging, which uses a tight weave, and open-lashed edging, which involves lashing twigs together to construct an open fence style. Both of these structures can easily follow a curved edge since the stakes do not need to be positioned in a straight line, and they are surprisingly secure given that they do not require nails, screws, or glue. Both methods are derived from ancient practices of wattle making and knot tying. You can buy plant supports and plastic dividers, but why not use wild materials instead?

Woven Wattle Edging

There are two basic parts to a wattle edge: vertical stakes and horizontal weavers. The stakes need to be stiff and relatively straight and can be made from small branches of hard wood, such as bamboo, cedar, or pine. The horizontal "weavers" can be made from almost any small shrub shoots, as long as they are flexible (not dry), or woody vines such as Japanese honeysuckle, trumpet creeper, wild grape, or even wild blackberry canes. When selecting branches and twigs, I admire their charming bumps and imperfections. I am captivated by the pitch pine's characteristic epicormic growths, mini-shoots sprouting straight out of the side of the trunk.

The exact number of weavers to gather at a time is flexible, because you can do the weaving little by little. A friend of mine, Mayfield, made a wattle edge to hold in the plants growing into her backyard along the border, and she started with only 3 inches of wattle; she used whatever she pruned and immediately wove them: she used raspberry canes, swamp hibiscus stems, redbud and pear prunings. As long as they are just pruned, they are green and easy to weave into the top of the wattle edge. Over the course of a couple weeks she finished it at 10 inches high. There is no rule that says a fence must be completed in a day.

Mayfield also said that it is easier to pound stakes that have a pointed end into the ground, and she sharpens her stakes to a point at the end on her whoop-de-doo machine (chop saw), but since I don't have one and can't always run over to her place to ask her to please drop everything and sharpen my posts, I use the steel rebar pin with a point and rotate it to make a hole in the ground to accommodate my stakes. · **This project will yield one section of wattle, 12 inches / 30.48 cm high by 60 inches / 152.4 cm long.**

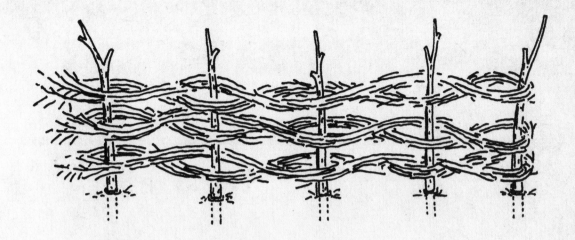

MATERIALS

40 long, flexible weavers of freshly cut flexible green vine or wood, optimally 36 inches / 91.44 cm long or more (the longer the better)

5 small woody stakes, 15 inches / 38 cm long and 1–2 inches / 2.54–5.08 cm diameter (substitute steel rebar pins if the ground is compacted or wet or it's otherwise difficult to hold the stakes upright)

Hammer or mallet

METHOD

1. Prepare the weavers by roughly stripping or cutting the leaves off.

2. Determine the curvature of the patch that you wish the edge to follow.

3. Pound the stakes with the mallet 3 inches / 7.62 cm into the ground and 12 inches / 30.48 cm apart along the edge line.

4. Starting from one end of the line of stakes, curve the end of a weaver around the last stake for extra security. Then weave the untethered end of the weaver alternating in front of a stake and behind a stake until you run out of weaver material.

5. For the next row start at the other end of the line of stakes and weave alternating behind a stake and then in front of a stake until you run out of weaver material.

6. Check your work as you go along, pressing down lightly from the top so that the weave is more closely compacted. Fill in any sparse spots with extra twigs or vine.

7. Continue weaving rows until you are 1 inch / 2.54 cm from the top of the stakes, or you use up your weavers. You can add more rows as you gather more materials.

Open-Lashed Edging

Lashing knots are still a common method used in Asia for joining horizontal and vertical bamboo poles at a ninety-degree angle for scaffolding. The open style works well to avoid casting shade and enables you to see through the edge to the plants behind. · **This project will yield one section of edging, 24 inches / 60.96 cm high by 100 inches / 2.5 m long, with two row rails.**

MATERIALS

5 straight branches or sticks for stakes, approximately 24 inches / 60.96 cm long and 1–2 inches / 2.54–5.08 cm diameter

8 sticks or branches for horizontal rails, at least 26 inches / 66 cm long and 1–2 inches / 2.54–5.08 cm diameter

Handsaw

2 large rubber bands (optional)

72 inches / 1.8 m of undyed twine, cut into ten pieces

1 pointed steel rebar pin (or digging trowel)

Hammer or mallet

METHOD

1. Determine the curvature that you wish the edge to follow.

2. Pound the stakes into the ground at least 3 inches / 7.62 cm deep and approximately 24 inches / 60.96 cm apart, following the edge line.

3. Measure the exact distance between the first two stakes.

4. Trim a twig to fit the area between the first two stakes with at least 1 inch / 2.54 cm overlapping on each side.

5. Temporarily fix one end of the horizontal twig perpendicular to the stake with a rubber band or fastener while you work on the other end of the twig.

6. Position the other end of the twig against the stake at a 90-degree angle, forming a cross with points north, south, east, and west, and lash the two together.

(continues)

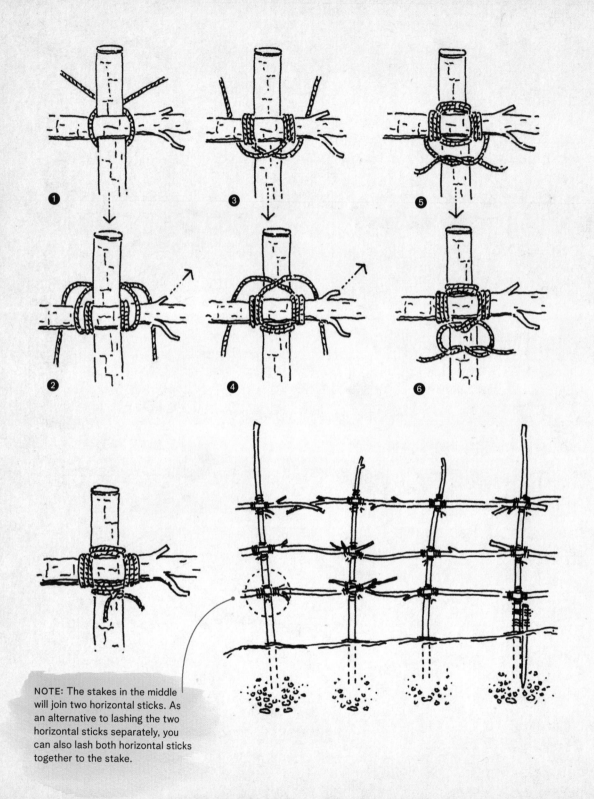

NOTE: The stakes in the middle will join two horizontal sticks. As an alternative to lashing the two horizontal sticks separately, you can also lash both horizontal sticks together to the stake.

Lashing two sticks together

1. Find the center point of a piece of twine and place it behind the cross on the south side of the horizontal stick. Pull the two ends towards you and wrap them up over the horizontal stick, crossing the ends behind the vertical stick on the north side of the horizontal stick. Pull tight.

2. Next, take the two ends still at the back of the cross and pull them toward you, in front of and over the horizontal stick, then down behind the vertical stick, crossing on the south side of the horizontal stick. Pull the two ends of the twine towards you up over the horizontal stick, and cross at the back on the north side of the horizontal stick.

3. Take the two ends at the back of the cross and pull them towards you and down over the horizontal stick, then behind the vertical stick crossing on the south side of the horizontal stick. Pull the two loose ends toward you, crossing them in front of the vertical stick on the south part of the horizontal stick. Pull the ends behind the horizontal stick.

4. Cross the ends in front of the vertical stick on the north side of the horizontal stick, then bring the ends down behind the horizontal stick, and pull tight.

5. Tie the final ends tightly in front of the vertical stick on the south side of the horizontal stick in a typical shoelace-style knot.

6. Repeat one more shoelace-style knot in the same place. Congratulations! You have finished your first lashing knot.

SIGNS AND LABELS

Signs and labels draw attention, sometimes in unanticipated ways. I use labels when I plant an herb or vegetable and I want a weatherproof way to remember what is there and what to anticipate from the plant. (Zucchinis? A certain variety of super-hot chili pepper?) There is nothing that says I can't also label certain unplanted weeds. When a plant is given a proper-looking name and handsome label it looks more intentional and less like a weedy by-product of negligence. In addition, it serves as a checkpoint for myself: ever since I labeled my myoga ginger (*Zingiber mioga*) plants growing in the moist shade under the pawpaws, I tend to stop and observe them more. The sign reminds me to pay attention. I use metal movable labels for individual plants. I write the name on metal with a weatherproof marker. They look nice and they don't blow away or fall over. I also will not disturb that labeled area until I am sure what will come up. So, if I scattered a bunch of coriander seeds in early spring, or lambsquarters, maybe I will mark the area with the label "LQ" so I can leave them time and room to sprout.

Also, the areas and plants that are NOT marked will attract less attention, and this can be good as well. We had guests over for a wedding celebration and I forgot about the walnut sapling growing in the middle of the rhododendron and blackhaw hedge. I knew that it stuck out strangely, and I wouldn't want it to grow into a giant tree in the driveway, so eventually I would have to move it. But since I didn't label it as "walnut tree growing on side of driveway," no one noticed it or commented on my negligent garden style.

There are also challenges to labeling wild plants, as opposed to trees, which are generally in one place for an extended period of time. At a meeting of a native plant preserve, an accredited botanical arboretum, a member asked why there weren't more metal labels for the plants. The answer: in nature, plants don't emerge in the same spot year after year, so the groundskeeper would have to move around many or most of the labels. Instead, they label the paths. The Marsh Marigold Path label meant you would see the marsh marigolds if you walked that path, though you might not find the exact plant in the precise spot next to a label. I also make signs and labels to mark the theme of an area, or directions. Examples would be Sensitive Fern Grove, The Swamp, This Way to the Pond. I have also installed Meadow in the Making signs on public projects so people know that it is not just a bunch of weeds but an intentional work in progress.

The bones of the garden take shape: plants of interest bear markers or cages; special habitats are highlighted, a wildish patch enclosed, edgings constructed. It's all part of a process of discovery of what grows where.

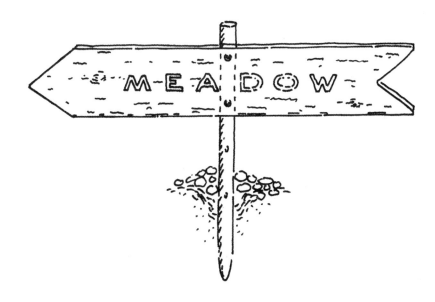

CHAPTER THREE

Connecting SPACES

"Three birds seemed to become one at the top of the sky. Then, in disorder, they separated. There was something wondrous about the meeting and separating. It must mean something, this coming so close that they felt the wind from each other's wings, and then blue distance once more. Three ideas will sometimes join in our hearts."

—YUKIO MISHIMA, *THE DECAY OF THE ANGEL*

ON VIEWS AND LAYERS 47

ON WANDERING 52

④ How to Make a Path 54

WILD WOOD GATES 56

Ⓟ Wild Wood Gate 58

Ⓟ Attaching a Gate to a Post 60

ON VIEWS
AND LAYERS

The experience of a garden, or any piece of earth, all depends on how you look at it. I can skip through garden montages like flipping through the pages in a picture book; I can also spend an entire day in one area, foraging, scuttering about. The garden structure should make it easy to wend your way, self-guided, through each layer; to trace the flows of the elements; and to be able to wander from place to place, between the marked places and by the edged enclosures, without struggling through brambles and vines.

The view from indoors: From upstairs on the second floor I can see an aerial layout. The separation of layers unfolds: the cut lawn of weeds, the tall meadow plants emerald against the forest backdrop, almost black at dusk. I spy on activities below: the flame-orange baby foxes emerging from their den, a doe sneaking along the fence looking for an opening.

The kitchen window becomes a terrarium glass, and when the passionflower trails up the window we watch the praying mantis, unperturbed, as if behind a one-way mirror; frozen like a gargoyle statue, poised to catch prey, changing color, grooming, mating.

A porch view: A porch is half in, half out, a zone radiating back and forth from the house.

Before I even step off the porch, I peek at the pots on the edge of the porch where I keep frost-

tender plants. Once brought outside, in these same containers I let the weedy, delicious *Galinsoga* and yellow wood sorrel sprout up in the pots.

Against the porch, rather than suppress the weeds with mulch, I let a little wildness grow: Queen Anne's lace, dandelion, wild allium, lambsquarters, creeping Jenny. Weeds can grow just fine in "foundation" soil.

One step off the south side of the porch, near the barbecue grill, sprawls a swath of feral mint and oregano. We did not plant these. Maybe the handful I picked from elsewhere and that my husband threw sloppily onto the grill had seeds and took root. The fact that the oregano grew so happily there clued me to planting other Mediterranean herbs in the area: **za'atar**, marjoram, thyme, sage (white sage and garden sage), as well as rabbit tobacco. I was similarly clued in by the chickweed and blackhaw and elder that grew wild on the north side of the house and planted lemon balm, *Magnolia virginiana*, and *Fothergilla* to join them.

Origanum syriacum, related to oregano but more aromatic, is used extensively in Middle Eastern and Mediterranean cuisine on its own, and as a spice blend, which is confusingly also called **za'atar**.

The view past the porch I think of as the walk-around zone, which extends maybe another thirty yards in either direction. This area I keep low and walkable. It has lawn grass in it, but over twenty years of never spraying, aerating, fertilizing, or irrigating and it has become a diverse landscape on its own: heal-all, wild garlic, wild yarrow, gallium, mint (*Mentha arvensis*), plantain, ajuga, spring beauty, and of course dandelion. How did these plants come to be noticed? In New Jersey I don't mow lawn grass until Memorial Day, when the grass has grown taller than my knees and is about to set seed. In spring, when the trees and shrubs and much of the vegetation are still dormant, the unmown grass area is the most verdant, with spring wildflowers and weedy herbs.

MANAGING WILD WATER

An area beside the house, just a stone's throw away, is where rainwater often runs, so I created a rainwater garden, which is really just a swale with wetland loving plants to capture all that water and hold it in the ground. The water runs fiercely into the gutters and off the roof during a storm, and streaming water also runs in a channel across the driveway down from the forest. The tall plants growing where the water flows divide the porch zone from the vegetable beds beyond. The channel curves and snakes, slowing the flow of water with the tall plants rising like a screen filtering the view to the vegetable beds.

Wild water, unlike water in a bottle in the refrigerator, is not just a commodity that is either absent or present; it has a life cycle. Fluid, elemental, tied up intimately with the terrain, the weather, and the plants that grow there, it is never fully tamed. When there is no rain for a long time, humans, plants, and gardens may just barely survive through supplemental water; when the rain comes it may come in torrents of rain and wind so fierce that the force of gushing water cannot be absorbed and it floods over, even breaking through concrete, steel, and rock.

How to Cope

1. **Direct the water flow away from the house,** from the impermeable concrete, asphalt, and plastic toward the permeable areas and deep-rooted plants. Impermeable surfaces do not let water pass through. And lawn grass, though permeable, has shallow roots and does not hold water well. The water will pool on top or run off, gaining speed as volume increases. But if you direct this runoff to deep-rooted plants in permeable soil, the plants will hold and store this water; the plant roots will also hold the soil so that it is not carried away by rushing water (erosion). This strategy can work both for the too wet areas that almost never dry out and the too dry areas, which are prone to flooding when it does suddenly rain.

2. **Slow down the flow.** Once a narrow channel of overflow water moves at least a few feet away from the house, the rushing water should be given room to spread out and dissipate, as our roof runoff does into the gentle slope of the floodplain toward our creek. The swale meanders in a gentle curve, which further slows the channel of water.

Start to follow where the wild water runs from and runs to. When it rains, watch for where the water runs off the roofs of buildings, and where the downspouts empty. If the downspouts connect to an urban sewer pipe, some local townships offer assistance in disconnecting them in order to decrease the volume of water oversaturating the community stormwater system. Look for other channels of water crossing your land.

HORIZONTAL AND VERTICAL LAYERING

Past the rain swale and the weed lawn area beckon the vegetable and foraging raised beds, another layer of depth before the dry meadow and forest beyond. See the forest as a stack of layers: herbaceous plants growing no higher than the knees; shrubs of elderberry, hazelnut, witch hazel, and spicebush; understory trees of dogwood, viburnum, and sassafras. The forest canopy towers overhead: poplar, oak, maple. Different layers will form under other forest biomes. In nature, plants of widely varying heights grow next to, support, and shelter each other. Tall and short create separate spaces and are more interesting than wall-to-wall flatness. I love the sense of these different layers in my garden: taller native meadow plants juxtaposed over trailing sprawling plants, a *Cucurbita* vine, some tiny sorrels.

On Wandering

The fog is dense this morning and my mind is in a mist. I jam my feet into rubber boots and the door bangs behind me. I'm in a huff about my ninety-year-old dad's health care: unexplained bills, on phone hold for hours, sudden notices about the need to move my father to another ward, payments delayed for months from the insurance company. So much is beyond anything I can control. I can feel my back stiffen with stress. I try to swing through the gate; it creaks open slowly. I'm striding forward, but the path, the way it curves and moves, forces me to push the brake. I wind this way and that, following the way: through the pale violets, the dew dripping, the sheen of newly green life pushing up, up through the ecru meadow. The mist blankets me with comforting stillness.

I spend an hour or more out there. I'm not lost. I'm following the path, making rounds to my markers, making some adjustments, foraging wild herbs to chop and fold into breakfast eggs. By the time I'm back at the gate, the fog has lifted and my mind is also clear.

By walking a path made to wander, without pedometer or phone, change will edge in: the sky moves, you hear a breeze. They were always there, it's just that the way you walk when you wander opens space in your mind.

Even if I have walked a certain path many times, when a new day begins, I still never quite know what I will find in that hour. Paths open up a way to follow without your having to make a decision on which way to go. The best paths are not straight and wide like a thruway—the goal is to get off the highway way of doing things, to make space to give you a way out and time out. The best paths don't march in straight lines from the front door over lawn to the driveway; they trail around and over and under and through things.

The elements of a great design already exist. It just depends on our being able to adjust how we see things. And relax. The earth bends and gives, with a little randomness.

How to Make a Path

A path shepherds you safely away from where the ground may be too steep, uneven, or full of brambles or poison ivy. The route should be wide enough so that branches clear headspace and one person can walk comfortably.

Width

24 inches / 60.96 cm
(standard trail width)

Height

8 feet / 2.43 m

Frequent walkways

A path can be formed by just treading the same ground every day. You don't need to cart in truckloads of gravel to keep the weeds down if it is a frequent route.

Forest trails

In the woods, leaf litter may cover the walking path. Use fallen and found objects to outline the trail. Move fallen branches and logs and join them roughly end to end so that a path is visible. If the woods are very dense, a sign can be nailed to a tree to mark which way to go.

Open meadows and fields

Mow a path wide enough for a person to walk through. Now that there are self-propelled battery mowers, I am freed from depending on a landscaper's large-size mower to make paths. I also periodically go over the edge of the meadow with a weed whacker where I see lawn grass, stiltgrass, or other potential invasive plants. This helps contain the spread of these plants by cutting before they seed, and it adds extra curve and tightens the look of the edge, the separation of lawn from the height of the meadow plants.

TIP: A battery-powered weed wacker with a hedge trimming attachment makes clearing bramble and woody plants much easier.

WILD WOOD GATES

I like gates. I don't mean towering gates with padlocks and steel bolts. I mean gates that show you the way, that connect places, that are the entrances and the exits. A gate shows the way without needing a sign. I leave some gates slightly ajar; this says "Welcome" better than any sign could. A gate can also serve the useful purpose of joining a gap in a wall or a wire fence. Even if the fence is rickety, it looks complete if there is a charming gate.

Making a small gate is not difficult. Unlike making furniture, making mistakes with a gate is not an issue. You just drill in another screw or undo the screw by sliding the drill into reverse. The worst that can happen, barring an accident (please observe safety precautions!!), is that you will have to go out another day and grab more wood.

To find natural materials for a gate, I keep an eye out once the leaves have fallen off the trees and I can see the structure of the bare woody material. This drives my family a bit mad, because no matter where we are, I always have my head half-cocked the other way, eying the bones of the forest. If I see something that looks interesting, I will get out and feel it. How is it growing? Stiff? Pliable? You can often find downed limbs and cut trees after a storm.

Note: Make sure that you are confident that it is not a poison oak tree or covered in poison ivy (see page 70 for ID tips), and does not harbor invasive insects that you might inadvertently introduce elsewhere.

I plan a day to get a group together; the weather is brisk but not painfully cold or windy. We collect a fair amount of material and then pile it up. Everyone can help themselves to make their own structures to meet their needs. Later, on a cold snowy day or other bad-weather interlude, I move in on the materials and start playing around with them.

Wild Wood Gate

To make a gate to mark the entrance to the garden area as well as the exit from the garden area to the meadow, I lay out the structure. The post and two horizontal beams of the gate should be as straight as possible, because if they are too curved, the gate will have difficulty closing. The vertical rails of the gate can be less straight, and you can play around with natural and asymmetrical combinations until you like the look.

The vertical rails should be a little longer than the height of the gate to give yourself a margin of error; they can always be trimmed after configuration and before assembly. · **This project will yield one gate section, 29 inches / 73.66 cm wide, with 6 vertical rungs, each 24 inches / 60.96 cm high.**

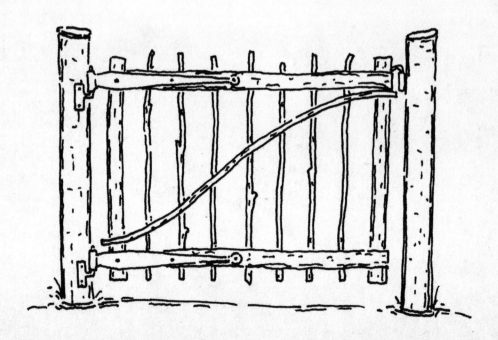

2 straight branches or small sapling trunks, 29 inches / 73.66 cm long and 2 inches / 5.08 cm diameter, of rot-resistant wood for the horizontal beams

6 branches for the rails, at least 24 inches / 60.96 cm high and 1.5–2 inches / 3.81–5.08 cm diameter

1 branch for the crossbar, 34 inches / 86 cm long and 1–2 inches / 2.54–5.08 cm diameter

Carpentry handsaw, 15 inches / 38 cm

15 deck screws, 2 inches / 5.08 cm

Hand drill with appropriate drill bit for screws

1. Lay the horizontal beams flat and parallel to each other, corresponding to the top and bottom of the gate.

2. Arrange the rails vertically between the horizontal beams in a pleasing configuration (see illustration for an example), with the ends extending 2–3 inches / 2.54–5.08 cm past the beams. The bottom of the rails need to leave enough room so that they are shorter than the posts, enabling the gate to open and shut easily.

3. Assemble the gate by drilling each screw into the rail pieces at the top and bottom where they cross the horizontal beams.

4. Finally, arrange the crossbar diagonally across the rails.

5. Drill the crossbar in two places to the corresponding rail.

Attaching a Gate to a Post

The post needs to be securely upright from the ground and preferably of rot-resistant wood. When I asked around, I got so many different pieces of advice about how to dig for the post. To put in cement or not? What if you don't go below the **frost line** perfectly? What is a shale bar? Do we need to buy a gas-powered auger? The one thing everyone agreed on is that the post must be dug in a hole about half as deep as the post is high. So, a post 36 inches *aboveground* requires a hole 18 inches deep at minimum. This post is designed for a small one-way gate, so I only needed one post. I wanted it to open on the right, which meant the post would attach on the left side of the gate. I made another gate for my woodchuck-resistant garden fence; for that one I made two posts, as I wanted to be able to tie it closed to the opposite post.

The **frost line** is the deepest point in the ground that water will freeze. Earth contains moisture underground, and when this moisture freezes, the ice will expand, heaving the ground and objects in it. Thus builders and constructors make sure that posts and other structures are installed in holes extending below this frost line, otherwise the structures or posts may become unbalanced or even fall over. The National Weather Service in the United States provides a map with indicative frost lines for different areas of the country.

MATERIALS

Manual post hole digger

Optional: Steel tamping and digging bar (also referred to as a shale digger), 48 inches / 1.21 m, to break up shale or other rocks and dig deeper

1 quart gravel, approximately 4 lb. / 1.81 kg

1 round post, 48 inches / 1.21 m long and 3–4 inches / 7.62–10.16 cm diameter, of rot-resistant wood such as cedar or pine

1 heavy-duty T-hinge, 4 inches / 10.16 cm long, plus corresponding screws

Hand drill with appropriate drill bit for screws

METHOD

1. Dig a hole 18 inches / 45.72 cm deep with the post hole digger.

2. Break up any rocks with the metal tamping bar or shimmy around and under the edges of rocks to crowbar them out.

3. Empty the gravel into the hole.

4. Insert the post.

5. Fill in the open space around the post with dirt. Tamp down the dirt.

6. Attach the hinge to the post and the gate with drill and screws. Make sure the gate is able to swing open sufficiently to pass through.

CHAPTER FOUR

Knowing PLANTS

 Dandelion Leaf Study 66

ON NAMING PLANTS 68

KNOWING PLANTS TO AVOID 70

IN THE FIELD: IDENTIFICATION TIPS 73

COMMONLY FORAGED EDIBLES 74

THINGS TO KEEP IN MIND IN THE FIELD 75

TOP FORAGING PLANTS TO SAVOR 76

Ⓡ Clammy Goosefoot Forager's Salad Dressing
(adapted from Amanda Cohen at Dirt Candy) 79

WHAT DOES IT MEAN to get to "know" plants? Knowing is an instinctive relationship between humans and plants; sensory, emotional, primal. Knowing plants means not stopping at the Wikipedia descriptions but going deeper to unlock secrets, because there is always more to know. Knowing means experiencing with hands, eyes, brain, nose, and many times, tongue and gut.

A graduate student contacted me for a book she was writing: "Did you really find 225 plant species in your backyard? How many more have you counted this year?" Does diversity mean that having 500 plants in the garden is better than 200 plants? I realized that I had stopped making it a point to count the plants every year and had started thinking of plants less as a collection (the more, the better). In some ways it is better to start with fewer plants, just a handful, even one per season, and really engage, study, and know them. Start with any of the common ones and the rest will begin to fill in.

Dandelion Leaf Study

In studying the leaf of a certain plant, be it tree or herb, like the common dandelion, the order and geometry and diversity of nature is revealed. Look at plants as more than a kind of background music, a silhouette, the pretty fall foliage on a drive, trees to be identified on a hike.

Collect different leaves of a single species, even of a houseplant or curbside plant; spread them out in front of you. The dandelion is a common weed, maligned as the bane of a turf lawn or garden. How often have you really looked at the dandelion, close up? Observe:

1. **The shape of the leaves:** Are they lobed, or pointed? (Technical jargon is not required; just describe it as you see it.) The outside edge of the leaf: Is it toothed, smooth?

2. What stage of growth are the leaves in? Are they just budding out? Fleshy?

3. **Color:** Lime, emerald, purple-veined, multicolored...?

4. **Surface patterns:** Is the leaf heavily veined? Or are there just one or two lines running down the length?

5. Is the surface fuzzy or smooth?

6. Crumble the leaf in your hand and breathe in. What is the smell?

7. Rip a leaf into shreds. How do the veins in the leaf break up?

8. Sketch a leaf or series of leaves, or make a print from it by dabbing the underside of the leaf with a water-soluble ink and then lightly pressing it, ink-side down, onto a piece of paper. Look at how the lines form patterns. A line may look straight but then you'll see it's actually just the tiniest bit asymmetrical.

Dandelion leaves are extremely variable in size, shape, and outline. Although dandelions have a single taproot, the leaves may lay out flat, or they may be erect and lime-green, depending on conditions, weather, season, and place. At home, I find the center, young, erect, lime-green leaves to be the sweetest.

OPTIONAL: How does the leaf look under a loupe? Field geeks carry a good loupe, hanging around the neck, into the field. Loupes are for a jeweler with a gemstone, or a field botanist with a plant, peeking into the geometric microworlds of leaf, bark, and flower.

ON NAMING
PLANTS

People, across time and place, assign names to plants. Common names are cultural names. You can give a plant your own common name: the daisy-looking flower in Mary's garden. But you won't be able to communicate about the plant outside of Mary's garden or learn more in books about its botany, ethnobotany, or culinary and medicinal uses.

Across the globe, scientists and academics use a binomial (two-name) system to identify plants (and animals): the first is the genus and the second is the species. Each scientific Latin name is assigned to only one plant, so across the globe this system becomes a universal language to talk about the same plant. I have been a keen observer at some expert field botanist meetings where for seven hours a day the botanists discussed the flora of their region, species by species; that's when I first realized that not everyone pronounced Latin names of plants the same way. I was hoping at these meetings to get a secret takeaway for finally pronouncing Latin names correctly. So I asked the wise moderator, Dr. Gerould Wilhelm, why there were differences, and he said that while the rule of thumb is generally to pronounce each vowel separately, (such as *rii*, pronounced *ree-aye*, which I love the sound of), people can choose their preference because Latin is a dead language, so there is no one to correct us as to the pronunciation.

The other aspect of plant naming that is irritating to the layperson is that just when I learn the Latin name of a plant it seems that some taxonomist (a person that groups organisms into categories) has gone and changed it—usually, it seems to me, to something more ugly-sounding. I understand, taxonomists, that new DNA testing sometimes reveals that plants previously thought to be sisters, or at least family members, are now found to be unrelated (or, vice versa, family resemblances are discovered), so they must be reclassified. In the perfect world of my imagination, though, a taxonomist consults with a linguist with a poetic bent before deciding on a new name, and searches for one that lilts off the tongue and is unforgettable.

Actually, there is so much variability among wild plants that where to draw the line on whether one should be categorized as a different species or not, a different subspecies (ssp.), or a different variety (var.) is somewhat gray. The line is determined subjectively by a committee made up of learned scientists and scholars. So, there are some botanists that focus on

Brassicaceae or only *Chenopodium* and are known as experts in those areas, or of a certain region. For some species there is general agreement about what is included, but in other cases some factions don't want to accept plant reclassifications. Groups who prefer a species to be assigned to larger umbrella groups are nicknamed Lumpers; groups who prefer narrow variation in a species are known as Splitters.

PROVENANCE AND CULTIVAR NAMES

A number of people ask me about "variety" names, meaning a name given in the trade that has a lovely marketing-sounding name in single quotation marks, like the 'Autumn Beauty' sunflower. Varieties named this way are developed for the trade through breeding and patenting programs. They have been bred, often for ornamental characteristics (larger flowers, larger fruits) or larger yields, and the owner of the patent of the cultivar will receive a royalty on sales of the plant. Depending on whether they are native or not native, hybrids, or just asexual clones, they may or may not attract the right pollinators and birds, so I generally avoid purchasing cultivars; they sometimes taste different and I have a niggling worry about their edibility. (For more information on the use of cultivars, you can read Douglas W. Tallamy's *Bringing Nature Home: How You Can Sustain Wildlife with Native Plants,* 2007). The only plants that I regularly purchase cultivars for are *Phlox paniculata* (so-called garden phlox), because I won't transplant this declining plant from the wild, and studies have shown that pollinators are just as attracted to the cultivars, which have the same tasty sweetness.

Knowing the plants means knowing the types that live around you. Plants of the same Latin name, variety, or subspecies can grow taller or shorter and have somewhat different coloration and other variables if they grew up under different conditions or locations. Sometimes these are referred to as ecotypes, like the Northern Ecotype or California Ecotype. I can find New Jersey Ecotype when I Google-search for it, but it still names plants that I don't find in my township (pitch pine, box elder). So, what's the point? The point is that the indigenous plants already growing on your site are the best for that site. Why? 1) Local-ecotype plants are adapted to local growing conditions and have evolved over time on that unique site to withstand the extremes of temperature and climate; 2) Local ecotypes help preserve genetic diversity and resilience. For example, the sedges and milkweeds and *Zizia aurea* in the seed bank in Kingwood Township, New Jersey, are local ecotypes; I value them for their individualism, so I don't dig them out or pave over them and then plant others I bought at a national store.

At the same time, I see some species of immigrant plants that look remarkably similar across continents. These are weedy, unfussy to a fault, and often scorned as throwaway problems. The ones I'm talking about are not invasive, keeping for the most part to those places where humans intervene in the land (footprints, garden beds, farm fields). So, I looked into where they came from, and they are highly valued in their places of origin—it's just that this reverence didn't stow away along with them on their journeys elsewhere. But when I bring some to a chef who grew up or lived in Europe, Asia, or south of the border, *poof*! They KNOW them, often by their local names; they spark a memory of home, and of good eating. They just don't call them weeds in French or Japanese or Italian. And if you look closely at these guys, they are beautiful.

KNOWING PLANTS TO AVOID

It's a good idea to know what not to touch before you start touching. Hand touch is important to understanding texture, but many wild plants have developed protective armature, physical and chemical, for protection against predators. While some of these chemicals are aromatic and delicious, such as the beneficial chemical compounds in oregano, others need to be avoided. Some common issues to avoid:

ITCHING

Species in the *Toxicodendron* genus contain urushiol oil, which causes a weeping, itchy rash after contact.

Poison Ivy. The urushiol oil of this plant exists in the leaves, stems, hairs along the vines, and roots in varying concentrations. Poison ivy is common across the United States and also grows on every continent, so identification is important. Don't look to the color of the leaves, which can be red-tinged and shiny when first emerging, but turn green and matte when fully open. Don't look to the form of the plant, either, as it can stand small and upright, peeking up in a garden bed; or be joined by creeping underground trailers and twine up into the trees as a hairy vine, with no leaves visible; or form woody hedges like a shrub, with clusters of white berries. The key indicators in the field are:

- Leaves in a pattern of three.

- Leaflets with irregularly toothed outer leaf margins and smooth inner leaf margins. The story in the field goes that an old witch lost a tooth and you can find a tooth or two on one side of a leaf but a different number of leaf notches on the other side of the same leaf. Be sure to look at a wide sampling of different leaves on the plant as not every leaf will exhibit this telltale asymmetrical toothing.

Other itch-inducing plants are in the same family: poison sumac (*Toxicodendron vernix*), a small tree resembling staghorn and other sumacs (see page 93), grows in specific wet areas, swamps, and bogs east of the Mississippi River. The fall fruit clusters are white or ivory in color. It has a very high concentration of urushiol oil. Two species of poison oak are found in North America: western poison oak (*Toxicodendron diversilobum*) is found in the West, and Atlantic poison oak (*Toxicodendron pubescens*) is found in the southeastern United States.

So it is important to know where you are in relation to where the plant grows. Poison ivy is common here in Hunterdon County, New Jersey, but (not surprisingly) I have never seen poison oak or poison sumac growing here.

BURNING (*Phytophotodermatitis*)

Burning is another skin irritation that may occur after touching or brushing against certain plants and exposing the skin to sunlight, technically known as phytophotodermatitis. The skin doesn't burn immediately, but within forty-eight hours after contact, the chemicals from the plant will induce a rash or a red streak that may itch or blister, and then may turn brown like a burn. These plants are most commonly in the genus *Umbelliferae*, relatives of carrots, with white or yellow flower clusters in an umbrella-like ("umbellifer") shape similar to dill or fennel. Some of these cause nasty reactions in everyone: wild parsnip (*Pastinaca sativa*) and giant hogweed (*Heracleum mantegazzianum*) are both invasive throughout the United States. I have been burned by wild parsnip leaves, and no one else in my group would touch it. I have read reports on the internet of cow parsnip (*Anthriscus sylvestris*), Queen Anne's lace (*Daucus carota*), buttercups, and even citrus inducing burns, but I have never experienced this personally when touching them on a sunny day, in contrast to wild parsnip, where I was careful with my hands but burned in streaks from where the stems brushed against my arms. The entire umbellifer group is one to exercise caution with as other members are toxic and poisonous (although many are also delicious, if you identify the right species).

What to do: Cover up and do not expose skin when removing these plants or moving through an area they inhabit.

PHYSICAL ARMOR

Plants have a fascinating array of defensive armor to discourage potential predators and curious humans from getting too close. Here are just a few of the most commonly experienced:

1. **Thorns** are technically a sharp, pointed extension of a branch or stem. A black locust or honey locust tree or an autumn olive shrub will have extensions poking out along the branches that can be painful if you are not careful in handling them. I make skewers from autumn olive sticks and find that when I remove the small extensions, the woody part of the twig peels down easily.

2. **Prickles,** on the other hand, are growths from the outer epidermal layer, the skin, of the plant. So thorny rose canes are technically not thorny, they are prickly canes. Prickles are easier to strip than thorns since they grow from only the outermost layer.

3. **Spines** are similar to prickles but are more stiff. Unlike thorns, which are found on a plant where a new branch or shoot would grow, a spine can be found on the edge of a leaf, as with thistle, holly leaves, and artichokes, or up and down the trunk, as with the Japanese angelica tree (*Aralia elata*), an invasive tree originally from Asia that I often forage for the leaf buds. You need a handsaw and

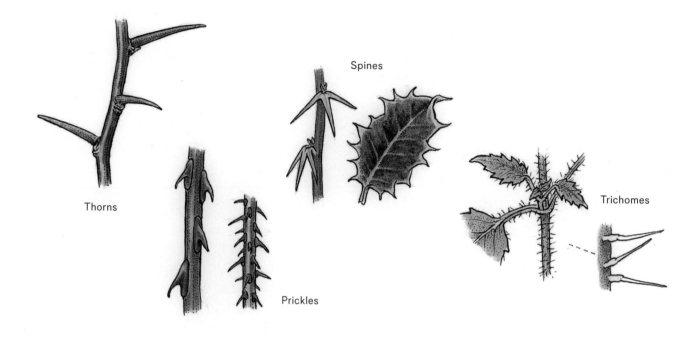

Thorns

Spines

Prickles

Trichomes

heavy work gloves, not light gardening gloves to remove spines.

4. **Trichomes** are hairs. The three most common plants I meet with these are:

- *Stinging nettle* The stinging sensation comes from hairs along the stem and under the leaves. I can feel the aftereffects for a couple of hours. I like the tingly sensation.

- *Prickly pear cactus* These are so tiny that you won't see them until you spend hours tweezing them painfully out of an ungloved hand.

- *Sticky willy (Galium aparine)* The most benign, they deliver a bit of a poke but not much.

POISONOUS PLANTS

The poison hemlock is a large herb (not related to the hemlock tree), again in the carrot family, with finely dissected leaves that resemble carrot leaves. Poison hemlock (*Conium maculatum*) and water hemlock (*Cicuta virosa*) are common, often invasive, weeds. Cases of poisoning happen when the hemlock is mistaken for a "wild carrot" or Queen Anne's lace, which is not poisonous. Depending on the amount consumed, ingestion can be fatal.

What to do: Don't touch and then bring your hand to your mouth, or otherwise ingest. Avoid plants that have leaves similar to carrot leaves unless you have complete confidence in your identification.

IN THE FIELD
Identification Tips

A good place to start is to learn which plants grow around you. I collected numerous books and guides of my local flora, including the now online *Flora of New Jersey, The Plants of Pennsylvania, an Illustrated Manual,* as well as *Trees of Pennsylvania* by Anne Fowler Rhoads. More broadly, the classic book *Weeds of the Northeast* by Richard Uva has photos of common emerging "weeds," many of which are by no means confined to the Northeast.

A state or local university often has useful guidance that can be searched online regarding identification and other characteristics of local species. The USDA, Calflora, Go Botany, and the app iNaturalist are sites that I use. In addition, numerous blogs, posts, and Facebook groups discuss plant identification, some of which are accurate and helpful, but not always, and among nonacademic sources I have noticed numerous posted and sometimes published misidentifications.

These different processes of identification may help to narrow the options down to one of two or three correct choices, like a multiple-choice question and answer. You may not be able to go further without getting completely geeky (looking under a microscope or waiting until the plant blooms, if

ever), but that's okay if the goal is to forage as long as both choices are edible (example: *Chenopodium*). The fun part is the dialogue, among friends and strangers alike, the puzzle of determining the dominant flora, the outliers, the invasives. No one knows everything about every plant; they differ according to time and place.

That is why *nothing* can replicate identifying a plant in the field, in your field, with its own idiosyncrasies unique to that land. To learn about my field, I invited a field botanist over to "botanize" and enjoy a sociable drink. I took elaborate notes of every word uttered. I also jumped on any opportunity to go out with local groups of locally knowledgeable experts, such as the Torrey Botanical Society.

COMMONLY FORAGED EDIBLES

Berries: If you stick with berries that are multicluster (several to one clump), like a raspberry and not a cherry, there are no poisonous lookalikes in North America. In addition, look for a little crown that sticks out on the end of a blueberry or huckleberry. Other than that, please use caution while identifying the plant before you pick a random berry. There are a number of berries that could make you quite ill (pokeweed, honeysuckle, wild nightshades).

Mushrooms: I don't "garden" mushrooms, although backyard cultivation is now popular, but I love coming out to forage for mushrooms; the mystery, the hunt, the potential "score." Timing is key for picking, as mushrooms quickly dry out and become tough and woody and often wormy. We look for pins. Pins are tiny, not even a mouthful size. If we spot a number of pins, we know what is coming. We just have to check the weather; will there be rain in the next few days? The young mushrooms, after the pin stage, are moist, meaty, and have an aroma that is savory-sweet, with a little bit of earthiness. Mushrooms are good candidates for drying, freezing, storing, and making tinctures. Maitake are my personal favorite for stock, but you can also use porcini, oyster, or morel. But there are a number that will poison you for which there is no cure, like the common death cap mushroom of the *Amanita* family, looking like the benign toadstool of *Alice's Adventures in Wonderland*.

- **Chicken of the Woods (*Laetiporus sulphureus*):** Growing out of decaying trees as a shelf mushroom or on fallen logs, the colors can vary from almost white to pale yellow to orange. The name reminds us that its texture is similar to chicken, meaty and not slimy or crumbly, without gills. Using a hot-water brine introduces moisture internally to the mushroom, as opposed to sautéing, which retains dryness. Brine overnight in the herbs of your choice.

Note: Other wild mushrooms, such as a large hen of the woods, also do well soaked overnight in vinegar or brine. In the morning any little oak centipedes and other critters that may be hiding inside will have emerged from the core. Rinse before cooking.

- **Chaga (*Inonotus obliquus*):** Cut from birch forests, blackened charcoal on one side and sienna-brown on the other, chaga is rock hard and fibrous, even before drying. It goes by interesting names—conk, canker polypore, heart rot—and is not technically a mushroom but a parasitic mycelial mass. It can be easily grated and used like a truffle, or steeped in hot water as a tea, with a very mild, slightly sweet end taste.

- You can use cultivated mushrooms, but usually I find the wild mushrooms have more umami flavor.

Evergreen trees: If you live near an evergreen forest, there is likely to be a mix of dominant evergreens there, which can be identified by checking regional guides and sources. Evergreens are also widely planted as landscape specimens, screens, and windbreaks. An easy way to begin to identify them (putting aside many hybrids and cultivars developed for nursery trade) is to look at the needle clusters:

- **Pine:** two leaves (needles) per bunch. Most common planted pine: white pine.

- **Spruce:** single needle, not bunched. Needle can roll between your fingers (round). Most common planted spruce: Norway spruce (the boughs hang down in an arc). Blue spruce is also commonly planted; the needles have a bluish tint.

- **Fir:** single needle, not bunched. The needle is flat and doesn't roll easily. Common Christmas trees are Douglas fir and balsam fir.

Most evergreens are edible: the new, light-green tips in the spring are soft and have a piney-citrusy flavor. (See recipe for Spruce Tip Mocktail, page 192.) The mature needles can be dried and ground into a powder that goes well as a topping for meringue, in marshmallow, and even with popcorn and duck.

NOTE: Do not consume any part of the yew tree (which is commonly found as a hedge tree), including the plump red berries. The yew leaves are flat and spiral around from the top, not in one direction. Cedar needles are also inedible and off-limits for direct munching due to strong chemical components, although they can be used in incense and as firewood (see firestarter project, page 223).

THINGS TO KEEP IN MIND IN THE FIELD

Most of the time in the field I don't lug books along, and internet service can be poor, so I need to keep some practical pointers for plant identification.

1. **Location:** Where are you? If you are in the New Jersey Pine Barrens, there are only three huckleberry species that grow there; that kicks out more than forty other huckleberries. And certain locations will have dominant plant communities. Once you learn these, the majority of the plants will be easier to identify. An online source that lists plant sightings (how many occurrences and where) is the Global Biodiversity Information Facility: gbif.org.

2. **Time:** What season are you in? Although this is not foolproof, since I just saw a dandelion blooming in December (in a sheltered nook).

3. **Structure:** This means alternate versus opposite branching structure. Opposite is exactly what it sounds like: the branches or leaves are arranged opposite each other along the trunk or the stem. In an alternate branching or leaf structure, the branches or leaves grow staggered up and down the trunk or stem, not directly across from each other.

4. **Growth habit:** Upright? Sprawling?

TOP FORAGING PLANTS TO SAVOR

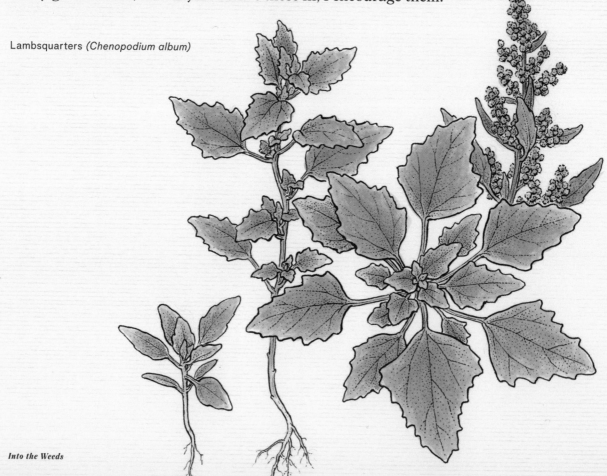

Over many decades, but most intensely in the last one, I can say I have come to know many plants. But the ones that are my favorites, that I return to year after year, are the following common plants. I love them. They reward me with their spirit and fortitude, many delicious meals, and their easy-care nature. When it comes time to weed things out of my garden beds, not only do I leave these in, I encourage them.

Lambsquarters (*Chenopodium album*)

Lambsquarters (*Chenopodium* spp.)

Lambsquarters (*Chenopodium album*), also known as fat hen or goosefoot, is a common weed across the world. The *Chenopodium* family of edible plants, which includes quinoa—both native and introduced species—as well as the cultivated spinach, is a regular part of many culinary traditions. Lambsquarters is one of the top two nutritious plants, according to Michael Pollan, and that makes me wonder why people ignore it. I see videos of people trying a plant to see if they like it; they often tear off a leaf and munch on it raw. But lambsquarters does not taste at its best raw, and the waxy film could put people off. In fact, many highly nutritious wild plants are better cooked, for digestion and nutritional value as well as flavor.

IDENTIFICATION

The technical term for disturbed ground as a habitat is **anthropogenic**, meaning man-made or human-disturbed.

Location: Found in **disturbed ground** (garden rows, compost piles, beds, vegetable farms, beaches). Lambsquarters has been found to take up heavy metals from the soil, so take particular care to avoid harvesting from even potentially polluted grounds, including of course dumps and urban industrial sites.

Structure: Upright growth habit; the leaves branch alternately along the stem (in contrast to leaves that branch opposite each other). Each leaf is shaped like a goosefoot, but the colors and shapes can be very variable, sometimes more pointy and thin, sometimes wide and curved edged, lighter green, darker, or even reddish. The plant has a waxy, whitish film covering the leaves, thinner or thicker according to the plant; to test for this, pour water on a leaf; the water will form droplets and not soak in. To recognize seedlings, and not hoe them out, wait until four leaves have formed and they resemble miniature lambsquarters.

Harvest management: Harvest the tender greens, usually beginning in late spring. Farmers commonly lop and bunch the tops off the entire plant when it grows to six to eight inches high, as an in-between crop while their cultivated vegetables are growing but not ready. We, for our part, wait a little longer because we want to extend the lambsquarters season as long as we can. We let the plants grow taller, to about ten inches or more, then cut off only the middle center leaders and eat these. This action encourages the plant to branch out and become more bushy, yielding more side shoots so that we can harvest through midsummer before the stem area becomes too woody. As the plant matures, buds will begin to emerge from the top center of the leaves; aphids seem drawn to this area, so cutting the tops and throwing them aside discourages the aphids and encourages fresh regrowth.

Cooking: Lambsquarters taste better cooked than raw.

Heat a wok to high. Add 1 tablespoon grapeseed oil. Dump in 2 cups / 50 g roughly chopped lambsquarters and stir-fry for a minute or until it turns bright green and the texture has softened. Add ½ cup / 237 g water to lightly finish and let the water briefly steam for another minute. Remove from heat.

The green seedheads may also be flash-cooked on high and added as a textural topping for soups and in many dishes.

Substitute: Lambsquarters can replace spinach or chard in a favorite recipe.

Variations: Since at least Mesoamerican times, Central Americans have a tradition of foraging the wild indigenous greens, known as quelites. Although originally wild, the local sister species of lambsquarters, huanzontle (*Chenopodium berlandieri, C. nutalliae*), are now actively managed and grown; I spied some plants growing between the corn tepees in fields outside Mexico City. I found them sold in heaps at the fresh markets in Mexico City, and took a closer look. The plant was undeniably lambsquarters, with its characteristic goosefoot-shaped waxy leaves and mild flavor, but the focus was not on the leaves at all but rather the massive green flower/seedheads, large as a bushel of wheat.

The array of *Chenopodium* hybridization and intergrading will keep me observant for the rest of my life. At an organic vegetable and flower farm fifteen minutes away from my home I found some *Chenopodium* that looked several steps removed from *album*; I asked Lena Struwe to identify them for me; she, like most botanists I know, loves a puzzle. She gathered the seeds under a microscope and also consulted with the nation's academic expert on *Chenopodium* and the verdict was: figleaf goosefoot (*C. ficifolium*), and then I found at another organic farm compost pile, oak-leaved goosefoot, *C. glaucum* (native to California and west of the Mississippi). I am also propagating another native, pitseed goosefoot (*C. berlandieri*). The leaves of these other species are more delicate than *C. album* and are tenderly delicious as a cooked vegetable.

And finally: Clammy goosefoot (technically not a *Chenopodium* since it is now called *Dysphania pumilia* by taxonomists) is in the same *Amaranthus* family. Clammy goosefoot is a low-growing summer weed, found in gardens and organic vegetable farms and reportedly especially prevalent in California. The

growth habit is sprawling but upright. The leaves are alternate. Most distinct is its strong aroma. The odor is described in plant reference manuals as unpleasant, which I tend to associate with moldy, rotten, putrid. Although the aroma is indeed too strong to eat it raw like a salad green, and the plant is too fibrous, the aroma, a heady citrus-herb mix, invites exciting possibilities.

The queen of vegetarian cooking, Amanda Cohen at Dirt Candy, loves to blend it up into a vinaigrette for her Forager's Salad.

For this recipe, harvest the entire plant when it is young, before seeding, and when it is tender, not fibrous and tough. The flavor is mild and vegetal.

CLAMMY GOOSEFOOT FORAGER'S SALAD DRESSING

(adapted from Amanda Cohen at Dirt Candy in New York City)

YIELD: 1½ cups / 355 ml dressing
TIMING: 15 minutes

INGREDIENTS

2 cups / 35 g clammy goosefoot

½ cup / 118 ml sunflower oil

1 tablespoon white wine vinegar

1 teaspoon Dijon mustard

1. Bring a medium pot of water to boil and quickly blanch the clammy goosefoot until it turns bright green and soft. Remove immediately from heat and drain over ice.

2. Puree the cooled clammy goosefoot in a blender, adding the oil in a stream until well blended and smooth.

3. Whisk in the vinegar and mustard.

4. Add salt to taste.

5. Use immediately or store in a sealed container in the refrigerator for up to 3 days.

Common Purslane (*Portulaca oleracea*)

Purslane originated in the Middle East around present-day Iran but now can be found across the continents of the world. Mild-flavored and smooth, purslane is high in omega-3 fatty acids. I pop a tender tip in my mouth raw or scatter it over a green or composed salad to add texture and nutrition. Lena told me she doesn't like purslane because it tastes slimy (or, as scientists say, mucilaginous), so I take her some young, clipped tips home from the farmer's field we are foraging. Ah! She likes it.

IDENTIFICATION

Location: Found in disturbed (anthropogenic) habitats (parking lot meridians, sidewalk cracks, farm rows, garden beds) in hot weather, sprawling low and sometimes spreading in thick mats covering the bare ground.

Structure: Leaves are spoon shaped, fleshy, and succulent (like a thornless mini-cactus pad or jade plant leaf), arranged alternately along the red-tinted stems.

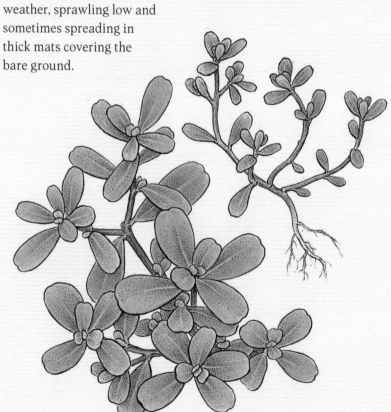

Harvest management: I've spent hours foraging this plant over the past two decades, merrily picking on a long summer's day. Knowing a plant means knowing when to harvest in the plant's life cycle. When the plant first emerges it has teeny-tiny untoothed leaves. Naturally you can eat them, but then that's it, you finished the season with no more than a handful. So I wait for the plant to put on more growth along the stems and then only pick off the top tips, not the stems. The texture is more important than the size of the leaf. Your hands will start to develop a fine tuning to the texture the more you forage purslane and get acquainted with it's growth stages.

When the plant gets ready to flower, it forms a bud in the center of a leaf cluster, usually at the end of the branches. This bud is shaped like the tip of a spear, very pointy; when you eat it, the texture is not soft, there is something pointy in your mouth. Most chefs I work with like purslane tips before the pointy buds form, but one of them likes the pointiness... I guess it depends on what you eat it with. Gabe, the pointy-purslane-loving chef, likes to scatter purslane tips floating on top of a purée like pea soup for extra texture to balance out the smoothness of the soup. Otherwise, the succulent-like smoothness of the leaves is very pleasant, with a slightly crunchy texture.

The sliminess starts when the stems get very mature, thick, and, yes, mucilaginous. I do not cut the mature stems because of this, but also because if I cut off only the tips, the plant regrows fresh new leaves and branching parts.

Cooking: Purslane is good cooked or raw. I personally prefer the tips raw and crunchy, although you can also just pick individual leaves only, particularly if the plant is too mature. Scatter the leaves or tips over chicken salad, guacamole, and salads—they're so pretty, crunchy, and healthy!

Substitute for diced green peppers in a favorite recipe.

Common Dandelion (*Taraxacum officinale*)

Originating in Eurasia but now spreading good feelings around the world, the dandelion (Jap. *tanpopo*, Fr. *pissenlit*) is a recognizable icon everywhere. And even if, in many an American backyard, it is famous only as a weed to be eradicated, not everyone feels that way. I happened to be delivering into the prep kitchen of a multi-Michelin-starred restaurant, and was treated to a parade of purveyors who had come to introduce their passion products to the chefs in hopes that an ingredient would spark a chord and find its way onto the seasonal menu. That day a group was in town from Italy, very excited about their honey. We all tasted the honey. It was truly lovely, with a silky, sunny flavor. They said this honey was extremely special because it is single-blossom honey, almost impossible to produce unless you can find a hillside completely covered with one dominant special flower. Can you guess which one? With supreme pride they brought out a large photograph of an Alpine hillside where the bees would forage. It was completely covered with yellow dandelion flowers. "Have you ever seen anything like this?" they exclaimed. It was very beautiful, but

inside I had to chuckle because I have seen something like this on suburban lawns where the homeowners would be considered "neglectful."

IDENTIFICATION

Location: Backyard lawns, vegetable and garden beds, other disturbed (anthropogenic) habitats.

Structure: The leaves are highly variable in shape, sometimes toothed and jagged, sometimes not; the leaves join at the center in a rosette growing from a long taproot. The golden flowers (actually a packed cluster of tiny yellow florets typical of plants in the *Asteraceae* family) perch atop a hollow stem; the stem exudes a milky sap when cut. The spherical white seedheads with silky parachutes carry the brown seeds away with the wind. The dandelion is listed as a biannual, but in some places and circumstances it behaves more like a perennial.

Harvest management: When people say that dandelion greens are too bitter, it is more likely, unless they eat only very sweet, bland foods, that they are harvesting them at the wrong time. The basal rosette leaves that linger, and often overwinter, can be fibrous and concentrated in flavor (bitter). Also, after flowering, the sugars will be largely spent on sweet flower production and the leaves no longer as sweet and tender. The prime time for dandelion leaf harvest is when the center of the rosette produces new young leaves. Select plants with center leaves that stick straight up and away from the older basal leaves that still fan out close to the soil. These young, lighter-green leaves are tender and sweet.

The roots and button where the leaves join are also edible, though I find grinding the roots or digging out the button too taxing for me, but I know people who love to fiddle with these.

My favorite part of the dandelion to harvest is the yellow head. The flowers close up without sunshine, on a cloudy day, or in the refrigerator, so if I want them open, I pick right before frying or hold them pressed open with a plate. They will also last a few days if I put them open in a plastic bag and vacuum-seal them in place.

Cooking: Dandelions have a long culinary and medicinal history. Younger dandelion leaves are delicious raw or cooked, chopped, and folded into eggs, braised dishes, and soups. Dandelion flowers are great in jam or fried tempura-style.

Substitute the greens for arugula or parsley.

Wild Broccoli Rabe and Mustards (*Brassicaceae*)

The brassicas are the family of mustards and cabbages and a major source of vegetables farmed and foraged across the globe today. There are hundreds of species, and these species also readily hybridize and backcross to produce new varieties.

The original species of *Brassicaceae* include two closely related groups that line grocery store produce shelves: *Brassica oleracea,* including cabbages, kale, Brussels sprouts, broccoli, and cauliflower; and *Brassica rapa,* which gives us bok choy, mizuna, and turnips, among others.

IDENTIFICATION

Location: Wild broccoli rabe or wild field mustard is found in fallow farm fields and on roadsides in the early to late spring. Although most of the *Brassica rapa* growing in the United States has gone feral from cultivated turnips from Europe and the Caucasus region, over generations the turnip root has disappeared as it reverts to its wild ways. In Japan today it is wild as well as cultivated for the leaves, buds, and flowers. In the spring, the *nanohaha* is beautifully packaged in bundles in all the grocery stores to honor the season.

Structure: *Brassica rapa* is an upright herb growing from a central leader. The leaves have a smooth, waxy, cabbage sheen and a clasping leaf around the stem. This plant is not as bitter as other wild mustards and is still tasty after flowering. Many other wild mustards are too fibrous and bitter after flowering.

Harvest management: The plant is a winter annual, so the first rosette will emerge in the winter, then go dormant, but is ready to shoot up at the first signs of spring. The central leader stem (apical bud) can be cut first. This encourages juicy side shoots (axillary buds) to grow from the sides of the stem. After the first pass at the central shoots, we return again to cut the side shoots for a double and extended harvest. The season can be extremely short, for if there is a warm spell, within twenty-four hours the plant may become too fibrous and the leaves shrunken. The plant behaves differently in different *terroir*, such as in western Mexico, where it behaves more like a perennial and seeds are sown in the fall to be harvested all winter.

Cooking: Remove any woody parts (knife will not slice through cleanly) and roughly chop. Can be prepared grilled, blanched, or sautéed.

Substitute for broccoli rabe.

learn quickly and are happy to teach their parents the difference between a heart-shaped leaf (sorrel) and a teardrop-shaped leaf (clover) in groups of three. By the way, if you make a mistake and eat a clover leaf, it is edible and won't harm you, it just tastes vaguely like cardboard.

Harvest management: In the morning, before the heat of the day, clip the leaves attached to stems in bouquets, not singular. Place in a structured closed glass or plastic container with a lightly moistened towelette and refrigerate immediately. Since it is a fine native plant, do not kill it by pulling the plant out by the roots.

Cooking: Due to their delicate texture, the leaves are best raw and add a nice tart zing to a salad or sandwich, or on top of smoked salmon.

Variations: Western wood sorrel (*Oxalis oregana*) has much larger heart-shaped leaves with white to pink flowers. Sheep sorrel (*Rumex acetosella*) or sourweed, native to Eurasia and the UK, is related to buckwheat and I see it growing in the sandy acidic lands of coastal plains like the Pine Barrens.

Wood sorrels (*Oxalis stricta*)

The common wood sorrel, *Oxalis stricta*, is native to North America, although it has a weedy nature, with 1.5 million occurrences documented across the globe, on every continent except Antarctica. I have seen it flourishing on construction sites in China and nobody there seemed to know where it had come from. All together there are about 850 species of sorrel, both cultivated and wild, with a characteristically tart taste, and they have been consumed by humans for millennia.

IDENTIFICATION

Location: Sorrel likes to grow on disturbed (anthropogenic) ground on the edges of beds and under taller plants, with some slight shelter from sun. With too much sun it quickly goes to seed.

Structure: Oxalis is easily identified by third-graders who I often hold workshops for: they

Chickweed (*Stellaria media*)

This is my own special plant. I am disappointed that it is called chickweed. Gardeners rip it out but it really is a fairly benign plant ecologically. Luckily, I am in good company: in France it is *la stellaire*, the little star, and in Japan it is called *hakobe*, one of the seven "precious" foraging herbs of spring.

IDENTIFICATION

Location: Open, disturbed (anthropogenic) ground near places humans go.

Structure: You'll know it by its low, sprawling nature, a little mesh of a mat. Soft leaves, coming to a point, sitting opposite each other on the stem. Flowers are white, small, and star-shaped.

Harvest management: The texture and flavor of chickweed can vary greatly depending on the immediate surroundings. If it is too exposed to wind and harsh sun on the crack of a sidewalk or a hilly farm field, the leaves will be more fibrous and withered, reflecting its rough environment. If sheltered from harsh weather, such as on the side of or under a larger plant or structure, the leaves will be fleshier and more tender. I select these more sheltered plants and clip the tips regularly throughout the cool weather season. Chickweed will continue to sprout new growth. It keeps really well in the refrigerator, since it is so hardy. Remove and do not pick the potentially toxic lookalike orange-flowered scarlet pimpernel.

Cooking: Can be eaten raw, or steamed for a few seconds. Chefs love the mild and fresh green flavor chickweed adds to a dish.

Substitute for spinach or microgreens, with eggs, on a bruschetta, or with noodles.

Regional substitutes: In California and the West, look for miner's lettuce, a prolific native herb also known as winter purslane.

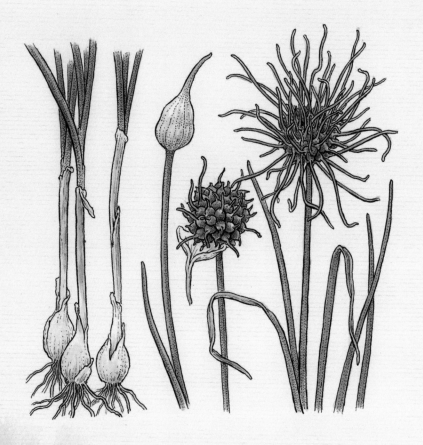

Although more commonly referred to as wild garlic, I consider this plant to be closer to a chive because the underground bulb is too small and fibrous for a good garlic substitute, although the aboveground bulbets are tiny, sweet, and delicious.

Wild Chives (*Allium* spp.)

Allium is a genus with hundreds of different species, many of them edible. Cultivated alliums we know include onion, garlic, scallion, leek, chives. All of them are perennials that return each year, unless of course the bulbs are dug up and consumed like farm onions. Chives, on the other hand, focus on the green tops and flowers, which are snipped and so don't need to be replanted. Scallions, if the bulbs are saved, can be planted in water on the windowsill and potted, and will regrow from the bulb. This is all by way of introduction to the wild onion: the common onion grass, wild field garlic, or crow garlic of European origin, *Allium vineale*.

IDENTIFICATION

Location: This wild onion can often be found in patchy lawns, open fields, and forest edges on disturbed (anthropogenic) ground.

Structure: The blades of onion grass are round, not flat like a grass, but the quick and easy way to ID is to tear off a handful: it will smell unmistakably oniony.

Harvest management: Harvest the aboveground greens in early spring or late fall, tugging by hand firmly but with a quick motion; the fresh green blades will come away, leaving most of the withered brown blades behind. The same area can also have wispy thin-bladed plants that taste mild and sweet. These are great for snipping with scissors as a substitute for chives. Other plants start from the earth right away thick-bladed, with a sharp bite to the flavor, and are better for cooking.

In early summer the green blades shoot up vertically and grow aerial bulblets, red-wine-colored globes. The germination rate of these bulbils or bulblets (botanists say it is correct to use either term) has been studied because grain farmers worry that thousands of oniony little bulbs making more plants and mixing in with grain will spoil the flavor. The key to harvesting the aerial bulbils is timing. If too immature, the globes will be fused together and won't split apart. If too mature, the bulblets will be dry and fibrous, losing their glossy color.

Cooking: I like young bulblets in salads and the older ones baked into biscuits and scones.

Substitute the fresh wispy green blades for chives, and the thick-bladed, sharper-tasting blades for scallions. Aerial bulblets are similar to garlic. The belowground bulbs are too fibrous for me to work with.

Variations: There are other natives, some rare in areas, and not found on disturbed ground.

The best known is the wild ramp: *Allium tricoccum*. At first, when I found out that ramps were a thing that foodies associated with spring, I gnashed my teeth. This is because I know these as specialized native plants. They are ephemerals, growing only under certain conditions in rich deciduous woods, mostly undisturbed. They also grow aboveground for only about a month; when the forest leaves out, they die back and store nutrients absorbed during that brief window back into their bulbs. When hordes of people carelessly go at a ramp patch, stomping around and digging up bulbs by the thousands, about five hundred US tons a year, the ramp habitat as well as regeneration is threatened. As with other alliums, they do not regrow if you dig the bulb (I hardly see any seeding anymore, and harvesters are digging them younger and younger). I was not able to make any dent in the number of people clamoring to eat ramps in the spring, so instead of the bulbs, I offered ramp leaves, and restricted picking to one leaf per plant. Since ramps have two to three leaves per plant, cutting just one allows the other leaves to obtain sunlight and rain during their brief season aboveground. There are many other kinds of oniony bulbs available, so we don't need to decimate the bulbs to get the sweetly garlicky flavor. Use the leaves in pesto, grill them, or make my favorite, ramp leaf wraps.

America; it's also found in Europe, Africa, Asia, and Australasia.

Structure: The plant begins by growing low and close together with leaves opposite each other on the stem; it's super easy to identify once it flowers, since the flower looks like a dainty daisy (a relative), and has stunted petals of white around a yellow center dot.

There are two kinds of *Galinsoga* I often find, hairy and smooth—but I can't really be bothered to separate them.

Harvest management: When young, the leaves are larger, so if you want to eat it as a vegetable, this is the best time to pick for volume. I pick the top set of leaves and tender stem only. The flowers are edible as well but as it starts to flower, the leaf areas shrink. However, these mature, flowering specimens will quickly seed at the next rain, and another generation will emerge in maybe ten days. One plant can produce a lot of organic matter, because there are multiple layers of branchings, each with their own sets of leaves and flowers.

Galinsoga (*Galinsoga parviflora, G. quadriradiata*)

I forage *Galinsoga* all summer long before the first frost. I can do this because the plant continuously reseeds itself (it is also called quickweed, Peruvian daisy, and many other common names). Its life cycle nearly follows a bimonthly cycle. Last summer, hurricane rains and 99 percent humidity made it tough for farm crops, but the *Galinsoga* kept coming back, even after being mowed down.

IDENTIFICATION

Location: *Galinsoga* needs disturbed (anthropogenic) ground. On routinely disturbed ground, such as garden beds or organic farms, the plant can be found swarming between cultivated plants in North

Cooking: Sauté on high heat. Originally from Central and South America, *Galinsoga* is a culinary heavyweight; the dried leaves are an essential part of Colombian cooking, imparting a flavor like an intense wild artichoke to their chicken and potato soup, *ajiaco*. Also known as *guacas*, it is much prized but only found dried in specialty stores in the United States.

Substitute for green vegetables, spinach.

Nettle (*Urtica dioica*)

For foragers, stinging nettle (*Urtica dioica*) conjures a hallowed image, like a goddess. I can tell in the way we herb gleaners say the word that nettle is not a trifle. Ahhhh, nettle! The aroma of nettle is a deep, heady elixir. You can find me settled in a nettle patch for hours during the months of March till May; the smell of nettle is the smell of spring.

IDENTIFICATION

Location: Often found on the edges of moist woods or fields.

Structure: Growth pattern is upright; the leaves are crinkly, growing opposite each other on the stem. Most distinct feature: the leaves and most stems have fine, hollow hairs (trichomes; see page 72). When touched, the hairs "sting" like little needles, injecting a histamine-like substance into the skin. I personally don't mind getting stung and think of it as activating my body's immune system. But it can be a shock if you grab a bunch and aren't prepared.

Harvest management: Wearing gloves, clip the top two or four tender tips of the young nettle before it begins to flower. You can tell when my group of foragers has been through a nettle patch: it looks like a large animal munched its way evenly across the entire top layer of leaves. Store in a lidded container with stiff walls so that it does not compress.

In recent years we have noticed that aphids become attracted to stinging nettles, specifically the part where the leaves join and often when they are about to shoot up to bloom.

This is when the sugars run high. It's difficult to see aphid nymphs because they are also green and hide, but a surefire way to identify aphids is to find a bunch of ants on a nettle plant. The ants collect aphids and bring them to certain plants, which become their feeding ground. So, if we see a lot of ants busy on the nettles, we go on to another patch. Of course, aphids are not toxic, and if you boil nettle or dry it (and thereby render the stings ineffective), you will also destroy the aphids.

Cooking: Nettles, when tossed in a pot of hot water, quickly turn bright green, are no longer stinging, and can be used like a potherb on pizza, in soup, etc. Nettles also lose their sting when dried for tea.

Substitute for spinach, green vegetables.

Variations: There are two subspecies (ssp.), the native *gracilis* and the nonnative *dioica*, which can be distinguished only after flowering.

Wood nettle (*Laportea canadensis*) is a different genus, found in moist open woods and floodplains in eastern and central America. Its season is timely since it begins when stinging nettle starts to flower and/or seed. The leaves are much larger and rounder than those of stinging nettle, coming to a point at the tip. In my area, one distinguishing key to identification is that wood nettle has alternate leaves as opposed to the stinging nettle's opposite leaves. I find it has fewer fine, stinging hairs (and it has some nonstinging hairs), and the leaf pads do not sting; but the middle, where it flowers and seeds, stings badly like a bee sting! Best to propagate by collecting some but not all seeds (wearing thick gloves) and quickly resowing. The flavor is milder than stinging nettle.

Sumac (*Rhus typhina*)

Sumac is a keystone in my world. I spend a disproportionate amount of time focused on sumac. I really learned about sumac in a deeper culinary sense from Eddy Leroux and Daniel Boulud (Restaurant DANIEL in New York City). They knew the sumac fruit cluster immediately and have converted to American sumac because of its superior flavor subtleties.

Sumac is such a survivor plant. I love its persistence and drought tolerance. I have people contact me from the Utah desert, where the cattle won't touch it; from Texas; from Canada; from China, where it is invasive. And of course there is its sister *Rhus coriaria*, from the Middle East and Mediterranean, cultivated extensively in Turkey on the dry slopes.

IDENTIFICATION

Location: Sumac likes to grow on well-drained ground. In the Eastern United States, this often means south-facing slopes, not good for tilling but fine for pasture (dairy). The plants like to be on the edge of a canopy. This is ground that is steadily losing "wildness." Hedgerows are tilled down, or hayed, or turned into lawn.

Structure: Sumac, like other smaller understory trees such as elder, grows from suckering roots. So, what looks like one huge patch might be just one mama tree. Over time the original center dies, in anywhere from eighteen months to several years, and the suckers grow fast. Sumac

leaf formations are pinnately compound and made up of long leaflets alternating on the central stalk. These can look very similar to tree of heaven (*Ailanthus altissima*) as well as black walnut trees, but neither will produce the characteristic red clusters.

Harvest management: Over the past fifteen years, the timing for harvest has been a moving target. I started out picking sumac in

September. Picking time changed to mid-August, and then in 2018 I missed the mark because we went away the first week in August, and when I came back the fruit was finished! What do I mean by "finished"? Browning and half-ravaged clusters. After peak season, the fruit clusters become looser and susceptible to heavy rains. Also, the last ten years have experienced a proliferation of insects which attack after the fruit matures to a certain stage.

Notice the red clusters. Get up close, push aside the outer layer, and look inside to the stem area. Is it whitish or whitish-gray? Not ready yet. Is it brown with weird little black bobbles? Infestation!

The most perfect time to harvest is when they are red through to the stem or 80 percent red. The color varies from place to place: deep purply brown, flame-red, brick; super clusters are "sticky" with sumac oil and goodness, an amazing concentration of flavor.

Cooking: The easy way is to dip in water overnight and then strain to make a great tea (see page 211). For long term storage or to make a spice, we remove the fruit from the stem and dry the berries, then grind and sieve and vacuum-seal them for storage. If you leave the fruit on the stem, there is a high risk insects will have a fine time in that shelter.

Substitute: For lemon or hibiscus powder; Turkish sumac powder is available online and has a more sour taste than wild-harvested.

Variations: My personal favorite is staghorn sumac; the upper branches are fuzzy like deer antlers. Other sumacs, such as smooth *Rhus glabra*, or fragrant sumac, *Rhus aromatica*, have not had the staying power or volume, in my experience, for making spice.

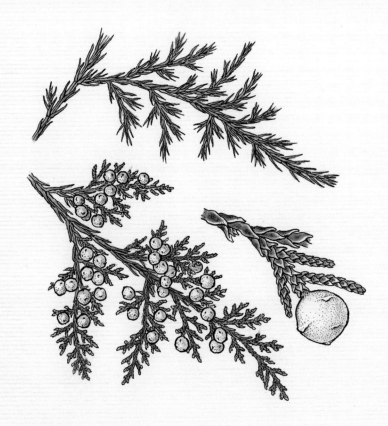

Juniper (*Juniperus* spp.)

Juniper is an ancient medicinal tree. It is indigenous and found wild around much of the world, with many cousins and species: *Juniperus communis* (think spice and gin), western juniper (*Juniperus occidentalis*), and eastern red cedar (*Juniperus virginiana*) are found in North America. Juniper is one of the key woods used by native Americans in ceremonies and also to make a hot fire (see the section on firestarters, page 223). At a landscape designers' conference, a speaker introduced a slide of juniper trees colonizing a field and explained how clients hate juniper and that it was almost impossible to eradicate. I thought I should go up to him and say I would take the juniper off his hands.

IDENTIFICATION

Location: Open fields, edges.

Structure: J. *virginiana* grows as an upright shrub or tree, in a cone shape, mostly in old fields that are not mowed. The needles begin prickly and spreading when young but become scalelike and flat when mature.

Harvest management: When foraging for the berries, I'm super excited to see a tree laden with these cones. It's not something to take for granted: the cones can take more than a year to develop, so there may be one or two "bad" years in a row; also, some trees are male and only produce brownish pollen cones. Finally, a large number of female trees produce very few berries. I have walked through an entire grove of eastern red cedar and found only one tree with branches laden with berries.

The juniper berry is rich in oil, and it can be picked green, in late spring, when underripe, or in the autumn, when blue/black. Pick the berries or clip off small sprigs for separation or drying. The berries stay fresh longer when still attached to the branch.

Cooking: *Juniperus virginiana* is much sweeter and less tannic than *J. communis* and can be used in a jus or sauce. The green berry is fantastic infused for a granita or cocktail, with its sweet citrusy notes.

CHAPTER FIVE

TIME *and* CHANGE

"The old solar agriculture...was time oriented. Timeliness was its virtue. One took pride in having the knowledge to do things at the right time. Industrial agriculture is space oriented. Its virtue is speed. One takes pride in being first. The right time, by contrast, could be late, as well as early; the proof of the work was in its quality."

—WENDELL BERRY, *BRINGING IT TO THE TABLE: ON FARMING AND FOOD*

FIELD RHYTHMS 99

SEASONS OF PLANTS 101

 How To: Meadow Doctoring 102

SUCCESSIONAL CHANGE 104

DEATH AND DORMANCY 105

WAVES, SURGES, AND ACCELERATED CHANGES 107

Field Rhythms

Spring fever. By the end of the long brown season, wintertime for me, I am distracted waiting for the reawakening of the world. The last days of winter sit bleak and dry, waiting for change to appear onstage, but not on cue, never on the official calendar day of spring. Instead, as one day migrates into the next, the season slides in; and after a spate of tin-colored skies, at dawn I see the light has shifted. This is the stuff the world is made of.

Can you actually watch a flower grow? Maybe. I think I have.

And just as the light evolves, perched on the edge of spring, one morning I see that the wild chickweed gleams emerald, where it has sheltered under the eaves. I begin clipping off the tips, these first greens of late, late winter (or early, early spring).

These days do not progress in a linear way, but rather in ebbs and flows; yet surely the spring light creeps in warmer and brighter. The chickweed stretches outward, and week after week I clip the tips as the plant continues to grow; I find myself, months later, still sitting with the chickweed, now mature with twinkling white star flowers and green seed capsules teetering on whiskery stalks. I catch my breath at a faint whiff of oregano and find, right at my knee, shoots of bee balm, *Monarda didyma*, a wild indigenous culinary plant I planted a handful of years before for the hummingbirds, and for me to steep as Oswego tea. As the sun passes overhead, and because I have been sitting in the same place for some time, I can't see but I can sense the bee balm inching taller; and after an hour more has passed, their tops are noticeably taller, above the

aging chickweed. Waltzing partners with each other, chickweed and bee balm, one recedes and the other advances. I crouch, immersed in the pulse of growing things. When you garden this way, in every place, one plant is poised to replace another. By the end of the day, in the gloaming, the edge between day and night, as darkness falls and the screech owl calls, shapes of the flora soften in the dusk and the foxes shrill in syncopation.

Time is well spent and lost in the field—and I don't mean by hurrying along. I mean by sitting on the ground, wiggling your toes in. Sometimes I am just about to give up and say it's not really such a good thing out here, the plants are meh. Until they aren't. Slowly and unintentionally, all sense of time and what was in your mind when you started off, changes.

The rhythm of a typical day: I keep farmers' hours, up at dawn, gear, boots, and hat ready; bags and bins, check. I am outside, bathed in the natural light of the backyard or the nettle patch or the mugwort. When on a forage, the first order of business is to do a minimal survey, but not a survey with a map. I mean ranging around at a lope to scout out the state of things. Are there large patches, are they easy to access, are they at the right stage of growth and not looking straggly? Skipping this step could mean ending up huddled over at one end of a long field, cutting a couple handfuls of purslane at a crawl, not realizing that at the other end awaits a massive patch of purslane (with the farmer desperate to keep it off the tomato plants). Scouting is also an important time for discoveries of new abundance or stumbling upon nascent pawpaws, sumac, persimmons.

Once I decide on the best spots for the day, whether in the wild or the back garden, it takes time to settle in: the first few minutes with the plants is all a bit off-tune. Even though I know a plant well, the touch of it, the smell of it, the hues, it still all takes readjustment. But somewhere in the process—it really needs to be about forty-five minutes—my hands start to work in a rhythm,

getting the feel of the soft, tender places to cut, where the best leaves are, the nuances of color and texture. I begin to remember from times past to gently tug on a tender shoot so as to cut deep, without digging, to where the shoots are blanched and tender. I stop worrying about how many handfuls it's going to take to fill the bin, how much there is left to do. A kind of bliss settles in; my mind eases off, no longer hassling over what I should be doing and what I forgot to do. Hands and eyes commune. I notice the colors as the sun ascends; a loose breeze skips by and moves the wisps in my hair. My ears catch bird calls and rustlings among the plants. The air is heavy with the fragrance of nettle: pungent, herbaceous, heady, a little mint, a little fresh green. And sometimes, not always, I become less an intruder and more an inhabitant; animals perceive me differently. Quiet in the dry meadow, except for the occasional louder snip, baby foxes approach, curious at what there is to glean. A dragonfly alights. Chickens and dogs on farms follow me around and loll about. I smile in their direction but otherwise don't bother with them except to sternly warn them away from my forager's stash. They are curious. Is this something good? They somehow feel a connection with my activities.

People ask to trail me for an afternoon, though getting to know plants doesn't happen in such a short time. The most deeply rewarding experiences, ones that are worthwhile, take time. These are times that build skills, build a life, and require patience and labor. So, if you trail me, leave your impatience (and the impulse to push a button, take a selfie, get entertained) back at home.

SEASONS OF PLANTS

There are more than the four seasons, as much of the temperate world knows them, marked by the calendar. For other cultures the seasons roll by differently. In Japan, they revere the nature of changing seasons because ephemeralness is life. Each movement is to be appreciated because the season will never return in exactly the same way again. And so Japanese culture has ended up with names for seventy-two micro seasons, such as Spring Winds Thaw the Ice and Damp Earth Humid Heat. In other places and cultures, people watch the skies for the dry season versus the rainy season, the cool season versus the warm season, the hurricane season, the tornado season, the wildfire season, the snow squall alert. A slice of hail for the day? As seasons get chopped up and mixed around, the world struggles to adapt to chunks of complex changes: the cool dry season? The wet warm season? Plant and human adaptations are necessary.

I pay a lot of attention to cool-season versus warm-season plants: Lawn grasses and agricultural grasses thrive during cool weather (60–75°F / 15.6–24°C). In the spring they green up quickly. They have names such as Kentucky bluegrass, bentgrass, fescue. Others, such as Bermudagrass, are fine in the warm season as long as they are watered and fertilized. (None of these are called weeds.) Farm pasture grasses are also cool-season plants: brome grass, barnyard grass, orchard grass. Cool-season grasses turn bleached brown in hot or dry weather.

But native grasses, what are these? In New Jersey we have warm-season grasses such as deer tongue grass, big bluestem, little bluestem, switchgrass, Indian grass. I can't even see a blade until after July 4, because although they are perennials, they need hot weather to shoot up. And, of course, there are all the other wild indigenous plants such as asters, sedges, rushes, goldenrod, and milkweeds that thrive in the warm season, whenever that arrives. My New Jersey meadow plants evolved to grow during wet, humid, hot summers in New Jersey (and the plants in your region adapted similarly to thrive there). Watching the seasonal patterns of the wild plants is the key to fostering resilient landscapes.

How To: Meadow Doctoring

It is possible to make a meadow by killing off all visible plants and then heavily reseeding the ground with a mix. Meadow mixes in a can rarely hold out over time, and viable native meadow seeds are expensive if you need to cover a lot of ground. But there is another way, one that capitalizes on the natural differences in growing seasons between cool- and warm-season plants.

Select an area:

I am not promising that a meadow can spring up from a dump site or ground that used to be a driveway and has been heavily compressed and compacted by cars. But, building off the learnings about place and marking special areas in chapters two and three, the first phase is homing in on the right area. The "right" area means the one with the most interesting potential for the least amount of effort and money spent by me: a place that already has lots of nature going for it.

Key characteristics:

- A "too" place—too wet, too acidic, too rocky—though considered poor for agriculture, can be great for a natural meadow. Special conditions may often invite wild plants (especially those that are indigenously adapted for a specific type of condition). Many plants cannot survive when flooded, for example, and need to be specially adapted.

- A place without a major infestation of invasive plants. It's easier to start with the least-invaded areas.

- A place where the land has been used with a light touch. The land has not been plowed or tilled, it has mostly overgrown lawn/agricultural grasses such as orchard grass or barnyard grass. There was no industrial hazardous waste dumped there and it was not compacted by heavy machinery such as tractors or cars.

- A place with murmurings of an interesting seed bank: walking around in a summer backyard, I spied one swamp milkweed and one ironweed. These plants reinforced what the land mapping told us: we stood on a floodplain of the Wickecheoke Creek. Most people would not be excited; they see raggedy grass of some sort, and bad soil, I mean really bad: standing water in the spring and rock hard in the summer. And yet, floodplains are venerated as rich edge areas that humans have habited as foraging grounds for eons, as with the great camassia fields of the Pacific Northwest.

First steps:

1. Mow the area once every two weeks until the weather hits 72°F / 22°C or higher. Adjust the mower to the highest setting possible (6 inches / 15.24 cm) so as to encourage clump-forming native grasses as opposed to sod-forming lawn grasses.

2. Stop mowing in July. Why mow high until July? During the grasses' peak-growing cool season, regular mowing suppresses the cool-season plants. Ceasing to mow when the weather gets hot lets in the sun, light, and air at the right timing for the warm-season seedbank to shoot up. Leave standing and don't mow again until the next year.

I followed these steps in my backyard, not where the lawn was lush, but where the grass was a bit straggly and some weeds were scattered around on the open floodplain down to the creek. Year one of this mowing regime was night and day. Where once were shaggy browning grasses, now there was a white sea of dazzling snow: asters of all kinds. I hadn't seen a single one before that summer, but now I know that these asters are some of the first plants that come up in a successional field. The purple love grass sashayed in between, a gauzy lavender glistening with dew on foggy mornings.

Year two of mowing: waah! In addition to the asters, I see more ironweed, and some dusky rose-colored statuesque wildflowers, Joe-Pye weed (fine native plants are also named weeds). I learned why I hadn't seen this plant before: the deer chowed on them before they got tall enough (this is when I introduced a deer fence; see page 156).

Now, more than a decade on, the wet weed meadow no longer follows the cool/warm-season grass rhythm. I only mow every three years to keep down any shrubs, roses, and trees (see "Successional Change," page 104). In fact, things are starting to get so wet I cannot mow in the spring at all and so just cut down any emerging trees and shrubs with loppers; I use the wood for kindling and structures. No more cool/warm-season plant distinction; the face of the wet meadow is now a collection of moist, rainy-season plants.

It is important to follow up with regular "doctor" checkups. Do not expect to "install" a meadow and walk away.

SUCCESSIONAL CHANGE

Just as the mix of plants in my meadow shifted over a period of years, succession is a common, predictable progression, particularly in old farm fields or weedy lawns. The tendency is to revert over many years to a **"climax" forest**. Unless young trees are mowed or cut from an open field, the field will succeed to a forest. And the early trees such as sumac or juniper will give way to larger canopy trees. But even within a climax forest, change is constant through fire, blowdown, or other disturbance, including management by people. Some Middle Ground peoples maintained different forest layers of succession for greater diversity and production. They would plant oak and then cut every fifteen to twenty years for wood and charcoal and to maintain diversity. I keep pioneer trees from seeding into meadow. So, in the wet meadow, pin oak, poplar, ash, and willow sprout but stay on the sidelines. In the dry meadow, sumac skirts the edge.

A **climax forest** was considered the last phase in a natural succession, but that is giving way to the belief that there is no ultimate climax because there are cycles of change due to storms, fires, and disturbances that open up the forest to begin again.

DEATH AND DORMANCY

Dying is a natural part of the plant life cycle, but people seem to cringe when a plant looks dead. Browned plant parts are typically not permitted to lie on the garden, but are blown by machine into tidy piles, debris to be carried away to somewhere else. For me, I delight in the Brown Garden. In the winter, or the dry season, instead of being hit with riots of color, things are quieter and still captivating. Shades of chocolate, Labrador black, and ivory; the garden is cloaked in a pale golden silence. And all this dead organic material paves the way for nutrients and breakdown for rich soil and new growth.

Plants that aren't dead but look like they are dying may not be immediate cause for alarm. My friend Marcia calls me: "The pawpaw tree is dying. It was full of pawpaws yesterday and today the fruit is gone and the branch is cracked. I think it's dying." "Hmmm, that seems an awfully quick cycle to be thriving today and dying the next," I tell her. I know from experience that pawpaws are weak-limbed. My daughter Becky can shimmy up like a young koala bear without cracking off any branches. She fixes at the top, the crown swaying slightly, the mango fragrance of the ripe fruit at the top. Any other less nimble creature will break off branches, but the tree doesn't skip a beat. So, it sounds like something on the heavy side climbed Marcia's tree. Something that likes pawpaws. And indeed a pair of raccoons stay in residence nearby.

When I spy some insects or grubs munching on a plant, instead of assuming that the plant is stricken, I first try to check what the insect is. I know that the caterpillars of the zebra swallowtail are crazy about plants in the carrot family. My mom's friend Susan texts me: "I have little green worms eating my horseradish leaves. What can I do?" I ask her to take a photo, maybe they are a good thing. She responds: "How could it be a good thing if they are eating the leaves?" Me: "If a bug eats a leaf, it can stimulate the plant naturally to produce more phytonutrients...I only worry if it gets off-balance. The grubs might be a caterpillar of a special butterfly...who cares if the leaf has a hole in it anyway, most people only care about the roots of the horseradish..."

Before giving up on a plant, watch for its cycles, the season, the day. Plants may seem dead but persist. Plants may be merely dormant, holding back, waiting for optimal conditions. Plants may fruit only every three years. We don't understand all this still (neither does science); the mysteries of why and when the change moves from stasis. Each observation we make, for a place and time, is important. Then sometimes you lose a species, and it doesn't come back. It only gleams in your memory.

Indeed scientists are discovering that eating stressed plants may benefit human health (the Xenohormesis Hypothesis by David Sinclair, Harvard Medical School.)

WAVES, SURGES, AND ACCELERATED CHANGES

Waves and mast years: too bad the calendar is not marked for waves and mast years. But even then, it would only be a prediction, like a farmer's almanac. Change comes in surges: ebb and flow of plants, wildlife, insects, fruit, nuts. Especially nuts. Some years I have to wear a hat or I get bonked on the head every minute with hickory nuts. Fellow forager Derek and I both notice things like this and looked up "crazy nut harvest years" online and found these are called mast years. It's a mechanism that trees use so that they survive by producing so much that the squirrels and wildlife cannot possibly consume all the nuts and more will be likely to survive. Okay. But when we thought about it again, we still had more questions. If oak trees supposedly mast every three years and beech every six years, then how do they know to mast all at the same time, even if the trees are different ages? And does it involve all the trees across the country? Or just our state? How large an area are we talking about? It turns out that scientists agree to disagree, and although there are many reasons (pollination issues due to wind, scarcity or too much water, etc.) that trees may mast or not, no one has "cracked the code" on masting. We had the most amazing local beechnut year in 2011 and haven't seen one like that since. Inside the burrs that drop from a mature beech tree in autumn is a triangular capsule containing, in a good year, a plump, buttery, sweet jewel of a beechnut. Nuts used to be a precious resource before anyone could just go into the store and buy a bag. But fresh nuts, in season, take a lot of work to forage.

Freshly foraged chestnuts are delicious. Since most of the great chestnut forests of yore in the Northeast have died from blight, we only find Chinese chestnut trees wild or planted decades ago. We wait until the green outer husks (burrs) crack open, and harvest the nuts before they fall to the ground. Once the nuts fall the squirrels, chipmunks, turkey, deer, and weevils quickly devour them. We try to get a jump ahead of everything else, so we hit the high branches that have slightly open burrs with a stick; the only time we have been forced to admit defeat with this method was to lose out to the Korean grandmothers at one municipal site. We all have permission to gather chestnuts, but these elderly ladies will hang out all day, about fifteen at any given time, reclining on folding lounge chairs they bring with them. As soon as a chestnut falls to the ground, like a flash a lady will dart out of her chair and stash it in a bag. When Derek tried to hit a tree with a stick, the grandmothers called the police, who came and warned him not to touch the trees with a stick. "You have to wait patiently like everyone else." I asked a young Korean chef friend what he thought of this, and he rolled his eyes affectionately: "I don't even mention chestnuts around my grandmother! She is obsessed with chestnut foraging."

We also harvest American chestnuts. My neighbor has a plot that is growing American chestnut as part an initiative to bring back the American chestnut tree by cross-breeding the American with the blight-resistant Chinese tree. But his trees grow only to a certain age and then, sadly, the blight still hits them. We found some young trees that do produce American chestnuts. The nuts are about half the size of the Chinese chestnuts, but the flavor is incredible: sweet and delicately nutty.

Change comes at a quickening pace these days. Bloom times are sometimes out of sync for flowers and their pollinators. I have noticed dandelions blooming in winter in a sheltered spot, magnolias in March. Others (anecdotally the indigenous plants), the penstemon and spiderwort, the asters and goldenrods, are not so sensitive and continue along the same bloom paths. Interestingly, weed scientists have tried to understand what is precipitating germination, or flowering, or certain key times for weeds in order to know when to kill them or mow them. Weeds, because they are so resilient, can be very unpredictable. For pigweed, the seed of one plant can have multiple different germinations and dormancy, so successful is it at breeding the next generation. I notice that chickweed follows *Brassica rapa* but precedes the violets; but then the chickweed is back again in the fall. Is this caused by day length or temperatures? The weed scientists say it is very complicated and "it depends," but one of the truest indicators of when a plant (for example, foxtail) is going to germinate is when another plant (multiflora rose) is blooming. Like a crescendo of the clarinet in harmony with the bassoon.

The truth is, I never know exactly what the day will look like. A decade ago, I could check the weather for the week or check my notes from last year and have a pretty good idea of what to expect. Now the weather forecast changes unexpectedly: there's supposed to be a downpour and then the edge of the storm band bypasses us, or it's clear skies all day and then suddenly buckets of rain for thirty minutes. The changing times require greater nimbleness and maneuvering: when I happen on a golden moment, carpe diem, before it surely passes, ever more quickly.

CHAPTER SIX

GARDEN BEDS

MAKE AND PLACE GARDEN BEDS 116

FILLING A RAISED BED 117

Ⓟ   Compost Bin Center 120

ON MIXING PLANTS IN BEDS 123

SHELTER, FENCES, AND ANNEXES 125

Ⓟ   Fencing for Garden Beds 128

Ⓟ   A-Frame Trellis 132

ON VINING 136

Ⓟ   Porch Vine Garland 138

TO GARDEN in the Anthropocene in the traditional ways is to try to maintain control in the eye of a hurricane. And similarly, to forage in the wild in a time of extreme weather conditions and changing land use chases the needle, looking for that elusive sweet spot. I long ago gave up on having a meticulous garden worthy of a tour with not a weed in sight. Also, I've found I need to stay closer to home and not travel too far to go searching. I've needed to manage things a bit more, so that I won't arrive at an organic farm or neighbor's place to find they just finished weeding out all the chickweed or mowed down the nettle. Unstable weather and changing seasonal patterns test the plasticity of nature and of our ability, as gardeners, as journeypersons, on an unknown trajectory. So I have come to rely on garden beds as a test lab to what works and what doesn't: wild and planted, native and cultivated, from a life cycle through production and on to recipe testing.

Raised beds are in fact a necessity for me because I live on a clay floodplain. The soil is too rock hard to dig a bed, and compost, unless contained, will easily wash away. Raised bed gardens are a kind of four-sided refuge for garden compost and plants. Even though their sides hardly contain the plants, the raised bed gives them a home base I can walk up and down, patrolling between the rows, checking. Each bed has a few dominant plants I am nurturing.

You can buy raised bed kits online, preferably of cedar or other rot-resistant wood to last a good many seasons. I also extend the successful enclosures I make on a temporary basis into raised beds. I reinforce the sides and heap up compost and soil on the inside of the walls, making sure the dirt is not pressing too much against the walls. The distinction between raised bed and enclosure is not a hard line.

MAKE AND PLACE GARDEN BEDS

Raised beds don't have to be confined to the same area; indeed if in different areas, they can represent mini ecozones. Some basic considerations are:

- Does the area have sufficient sunshine if planting vegetables?

- Will it interfere with a specially marked area with rare or uncommon wild plants?

- Is the area clear of pipes, electric wiring, tree roots, and rocks?

- Is the area situated on an infestation of invasive plants or atop a woodchuck den?

- Is the area mower-width distance away from other raised beds to permit easy walking access?

FILLING A RAISED BED

SOIL

I fill the beds halfway with local soil, wild soil. I also add in local organic matter such as woody bits, leaves, green plants, composted vegetables, and mushroom compost from nearby organic farms; these break down and decompose via the combined actions of worms, insects, and microbes so that over time they will create nutrient- and mineral-rich soil that is sufficient for the plants that want to grow there. I like doing things this way because I like to know what really is going into my garden.

FERTILIZER AND SOIL AMENDMENTS

Agricultural or ornamental crops, as we know them, are often heavy feeders; they deplete the soil and need these minerals to obtain higher yields. Some labs will also do tests more tailored to small farm vegetable gardens or to home landscapes. Indigenous native plants and herbs do not require fertilizing. Many wild plants thrive in soil considered barren or too poor for common crops. Also, a wild plant already growing well on site has acclimated to the soil conditions there. And, of course, to many farmers' and gardeners' chagrin, many unwanted weedy plants thrive in pre-mixed soil mediums as well as disturbed soil.

MULCH OR COMPOST

The technical difference between the two is that mulch is used more as a top dressing to control and suppress weeds and keep moisture from evaporating off the top of bare ground. Mulch can be composed of organic materials, such as dead leaves or wood chips, or synthetic materials, such as gravel. Some gardeners fill in all the spaces between beds or even plants with mulch, I guess to reduce the onerousness of weeding. I generally do not mulch in the garden, because I enjoy the natural plants that grow there as ground cover, as they would in nature. In this way, I discovered spring ephemerals such as trout lily and spring beauty, which like to grow around the base of trees, pawpaw saplings, and hen of the woods mushrooms, all of which would have been suppressed by a layer of mulch. Occasionally, usually in the middle of the summer, I do mulch under garden vegetables such as cucumbers or tomatoes with straw or discarded weeds.

Compost, on the other hand, may be worked into the soil to add more organic matter and nutrients for plant growth. Compost is also made up of organic matter, but in various stages of decomposition from kitchen scraps, grass clippings, weeds, plant debris. This matter further breaks down and, if you apply it to your garden, returns back to enrich the soil instead of piling up in a township waste management system. There are numerous methods that people use to compost their organic waste, and many people purchase a kitchen compost receptacle (I just use a metal container) or a composting bin that might turn.

Multiple mini-piles: No one says that you need to throw all your compost into a single bin in one place. Last year I was struggling trying to wheelbarrow around loads of plant material to dump into the compost pile and dreading having to wheel it back out again through the spring muck. I asked my friend Deborah, who has been composting for decades, how she trucks her compost around, and found out that she has a number of discreetly stashed compost piles around her place. So, once I got it in my head that this would pass as "permissible composting," that fall I stashed small heaps of compost in different areas where I wanted to build up good organic matter. I have two heaps in the corners of large beds where the soil is starting to get low. I also throw grass clippings directly into the nearest pile. This way I don't have to cart them back to the central compost pile and then cart them back to the bed area again.

A central compost bin: A "proper" functioning compost bin has always been my Achilles' heel. I've tried so many methods over the years that didn't produce compost. First, I bought a compost bin at a garden supply store. The bin was made of plastic and had a shelf at the bottom. We threw food scraps in the top and occasionally leaves and soil. This didn't work. The bottom "drawer" never opened because there was too much pressure from the inside, and it would not slide up. Also, we were not able to "turn"

the compost because we couldn't reach deep into the bottom with a pitchfork and at the same time have enough space to toss it around. (I have short arms.) In the end the compost bin itself went up in flames when an (adult) member of the family threw still-smoldering ashes into the bin, and it caught on fire and melted.

As my foraging produced more and more compost-worthy matter, we tried an open compost heap, in an area about five by seven feet. We layered green material (grass clippings, food scraps, weeds) alternating with brown material (cardboard, sticks, dirt), and it "worked," in that there were no smells or noticeable animal interest. The pile decomposed down and really cool things grew out of it, like pawpaw trees. However, it never really produced extra compost to spread to other areas of the garden.

Enter my friend Deborah again. She looked at this compost heap and said the problem was not that I was not turning it or making it heat up. That was a relief, because these activities would not be realistic given my already long list of things to do. She said the problem was that I kept adding new material on top of the old. She uses the three-bin method: you fill up one bin, and once it's full, let it rest and go on to the next one. When that second bin is full, you go on to the next. The time it takes to fill the three bins is sufficiently long so that by the time you finish the last one, the first one is ready to use. It could take as long as a year, depending on the weather. She also says that if the first bin still has bits that are not fully broken down (bits of sticks, etc.) she screens these out and throws the larger bits into bin number two. These semi-decomposed bits are good "starter" for the second bin.

Compost Bin Center

The following project will yield three bins joined together with two shared walls, 48 inches / 1.2 m tall by 48 inches / 1.2 m wide.

MATERIALS

10 pallets, each 48 inches by 48 inches / 1.2 m by 1.2 m

Drill

30 exterior deck screws, 3 inches / 7.62 cm

Rebar (optional) if extra support is needed around the outside. We didn't need this.

METHOD

1. Place four of the pallets upright to form roughly a square. (The shape may not be exactly square, and that's not a problem.) It's better if the slat side of each pallet (the part where normally the goods would be placed on top) faces to the inside of the compost bin. These top slats usually are of wider wood slats, so placing this side on the inside will hold the compost more effectively. Having some space between the slats is helpful to allow air and water to flow through the bin.

2. Join the corners of the square with the screws:

   a. The point of the screw should start in the thinner wood, screwing into the thicker wood. You always want to have the screw go at least 1 inch / 2.54 cm into the attached wood for a more secure hold. The screw will go farther if you attach from thin to thick, rather than from thick to thin.

   b. Drill the screw in for a couple seconds at a vertical angle. Stop. Remove screw. *Note:* You only need a pilot hole (a predrilled hole for the screw to go into) if the wood is hardwood or things need to be precise. Pine used in pallets is softwood.

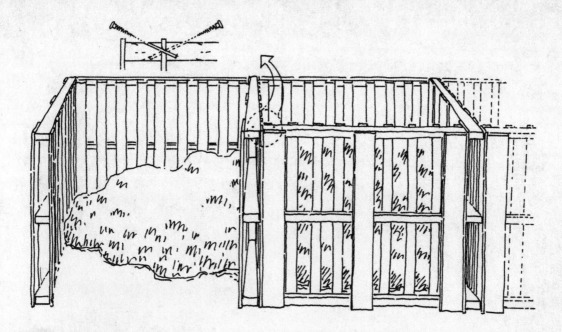

Since the pallets have to be able to hold together with a lot of pressure from within, it is better to use screws than nails. Be sure to get screws that are designed for outdoor use: deck screws (stainless steel). The screws have to be long enough to go through the pallets for a secure hold. The longest we could easily source was 3 inches / 7.62 cm, but sometimes you can also find 4 inches / 10.16 cm.

c. Place the screw back in the hole, but this time at a diagonal, and drill it in at a diagonal. This is what is known as toenailing for a stronger corner hold.

3. Attach three sides this way, spacing screws up and down the sides, three to a side.

4. For the fourth and last side, position so that the three joined sides face the way you want to access the bin. The opening needs to be easy to access in the side not yet attached. You want to be able to easily remove this side in order to shovel out the compost. Drill the screws the same way but only two screws at the top, not up and down the sides. When you need to open the bin, you just unscrew the top two screws by drilling the screws in reverse.

5. Repeat for the last six pallets to make two more squares.

ON MIXING PLANTS IN BEDS

A typical garden bed plan begins with neat rows organized by a common theme: a rose garden, a white garden. A vegetable garden may feature only lettuces in one long bed and tomatoes in a different section, flowers in yet another. I like to plan garden beds as well. Like any nascent gardener, I pore through seed catalogs in the winter, dreaming of eating plants that I can't find at the grocery store, Asian greens such as tatsoi, shungiku, mizuna, mizuba, as well as plants that aren't fresh enough for my liking at the grocery store, like parsley, dill, horseradish. I also want that sensation of picking and immediately popping the fruit of a plant in my mouth. Pick a pea, slip it from the pod: the taste is startling after winter roots and frozen vegetables. The raw green of spring, fresh and living—there's nothing else quite like it.

Plugs are plants that have germinated in a nursery; seedlings are often sold wholesale, or online. They are still young but the roots have developed sufficiently so that they can be replanted into a flowerpot or directly in the ground. Herbs are particularly suited to ordering in plug. Some vegetables I need to buy as plugs every year because they are not frost hardy, such as cucumbers, zucchini, and peas.

I plan the beds based on:

1. What things rabbits and woodchucks favor. I put all these in a fenced-in area. Since they never touch purslane or lambsquarters, I can plant them in very exposed beds.

2. Where there is part shade

3. Where plants have room to spread

4. Not putting all my eggs in one basket (I try out a new plant in more than one spot)

I always look for plants that I can't easily find in the grocery stores and that don't need a lot of care. I am not great at seed starting indoors so I tend to favor ordering a flat or **plugs** or getting seeds that I can scatter outdoors. I like to buy from specialty nurseries such as Kitazawa Seed Company, Richters Herbs, Baker Creek Heirloom Seeds and my local Taiwanese-owned nursery. I also order from Wood Thrush Native or Prairie Moon nursery. Look for your local native plant nonprofits for native perennials.

I plant these in beds and I let them mix in with wild plants of two sorts:

1. Top foraging plants that I know (see chapter four)

2. Native plants that are not edible but add depth, layers, or shelter: ironweed, milkweed, Joe-Pye weed, mountain mint, evening primrose, *Rudbeckia* (in my area)

Over the years, the number of beds has multiplied; instead of the traditional garden mode of creating well-defined beds of, say, roses here, spring bulbs there, these beds are a dazzling array of diversity; a mixed blend of natives and nonnatives, perennials, annuals, and biannuals. There is a lot of fecundity in these beds.

One of the advantages of mixing plants in beds is that I have few insect problems on my garden vegetables. The garden is full of little busy bugs, but they are not feasting on the vegetables. I have noticed that some of the usual pests, such as Japanese beetles, clearly go crazy for certain preferred species such as evening primrose (*Oenothera biennis*) or *Desmodium* spp.; if I let these native weeds grow up in the garden beds, the Japanese beetles don't attack the other plants in the bed. I notice also that these weeds have developed their own tactics; yes, the beetles munch on them during the beginning of the season, but the plants come back after the beetles are gone, flowering and seeding later.

I use some raised beds as experimental beds for plants, both wild and not so wild, that I had seed for and wanted to plant, and I call these nurse beds. The raised bed and a label help me keep track of something new and know what to look out for. One example of a local wild plant that is not found in nurseries is the American germander (*Teucrium canadense*), a beautiful, flowering, wet-loving plant. I figured if it could grow untended in the summer creek bed behind my house, covered by water the rest of the year, that was a strong plant. The *Teucrium* has thrived and spread out to cover the bed I planted it into. I have potted up plants from the bed and gifted them to conservation groups along the creek as well as neighbors living near the creek.

Another nurse bed for the opposite type of habitat is dry and well drained. Since most of my land is very wet, a raised bed helps wild fennel (*Foeniculum vulgare*) attuned to a more Mediterranean climate settle in. It is invasive in California, but it does not jump into the naturally wet areas where I live.

From time to time, I have had the following successes in nurse beds: sumac, native hops, meadowsweet, camphorweed, beach plum, rabbit tobacco. Now, after a decade, many generations of native plants are robustly established all over my property. They even pop up in the middle of my garden beds, so I just let them be as long as they don't take over, or I bequeath them to others. For example, common milkweed, a keystone plant for monarch butterflies and a mini-ecosystem for wildlife, disappeared from the dry meadow and is populating my large "garden" bed. I let it be there and use its height. Interspersing tall plants with low, sprawling plants can be very effective. I noticed at organic vegetable farms that some of the best chickweed and purslane grows where there is a bit of shelter from the hottest of hot days, winds, and intense storms. Many small, nice greens grow next to sunflowers, okra, and cutting flowers; they are low to the ground and so do not compete for light, and they help to keep the soil moist, add organic matter, and prevent erosion. Tall milkweed plants, ironweed, or evening primrose (*Oenoethera biennis*) in the middle of a bed have brought a kind of symbiosis into my mixed weed-vegetable garden. My garden is of wild and not so wild plants, with vegetables and herbs as a bonus. I don't see the benefit of an all-or-nothing approach, and I don't think the plants do either.

SHELTER, FENCES, AND ANNEXES

Aside from the shelter from taller plants in a garden, I have to work at devising additional protective tactics. Nature is resilient, but plants, even hardy weeds, can be stressed when temperatures fluctuate fifty degrees or more in a day, or when hail or severe winds blow in with little advance warning. Although I come from an attitude of letting things adapt to the climate, I realize that I need to take a more active approach these days, even just to "take the edge" off the risk and give the plants a little cushion.

Every year seems to have a new challenge. This year seems to be the year of the baby rabbit. All the neighbors round these parts are complaining. The little ones are small and wily; they can squeeze in between the spaces of many a wire fence (not chicken wire, though) and push away little barriers. I have no clue why they will go to great lengths to eat the entire tops off of cow parsnip (*Heracleum maximum*), not touching the cucumber or zucchini. The cow parsnip is a brutish, hairy-leaved weed of a native plant (the stems are delicious if the ID is accurate), but there is a limit to how many times in the season they can be nibbled to the ground before they die away. No problem! I just pop on a **high crate** and the rabbits can't push it over; it's easy for me to lift off to see how the plants are regrowing and to plan future protective tactics in the meantime. Crates are also useful for out-of-the-ordinary weather events like light frosts, heat waves, harsh winds, and rain torrents.

We save plastic vegetable crates from farmers and distributors. They are food safe and sturdy. Just as my mother would use the cut-off bottoms of plastic milk jugs, I use rectangular vegetable crates, like milk crates, with lots of holes or openings, where I need a quick shelter, turning them upside down.

Fencing for Garden Beds

Raised garden beds should already afford some protection from critters. Try to determine what kind of wildlife may be eyeing your plants. A deer will be able to reach the tops of taller plants, flower buds, and tree shoots, so you may need taller fencing for protection. Woodchucks can climb sturdy structures, so I make sure to use wobbly chicken wire (see page 28) or fencing whose top bends backward to protect against climbers. Rabbits can shimmy through wire fence gaps of only 2 to 3 inches / 5.08–7.62 cm, so I use chicken wire with 1-inch / 2.54 cm holes when they are the concern. They can also burrow and squeeze under gaps at the bottom of a fence. For pests that dig from underground, place a mesh wire on the ground before the bed is placed on top. If your soil is ridden with rocks and heavy clay like mine, you may not experience critters digging under your garden beds.

For many years I bought premade garden covers to cover the beds and keep out unwanted pests. These lasted only a year or two and I got tired of storing them when not in use. Now I make use of the existing raised bed structures by attaching straight thick branches or thinner saplings to each of the corners of my raised beds. These act like the corner "posts" of an old-fashioned four-poster bed, and I use them to secure wire fencing around the bed. The fencing lasts for years and I don't need to put it away during the winter. · **This project will yield 4 by 6 feet / 1.22 by 1.82 m of fencing for a raised garden bed.**

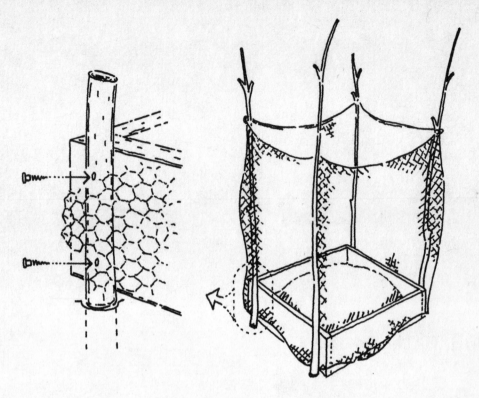

MATERIALS

4 wild pine sapling or other straight branches, one for each "post," at least 48 inches / 1.21 m high and 4.5 inches / 11.43 cm diameter

8 outdoor deck screws, 3 inches / 7.62 cm

Drill

Chicken wire, 4 feet / 1.22 m tall and long enough to cover the perimeter of your bed. (For a raised bed 4 by 6 feet / 1.22 by 1.82 m, this would be 20 feet / 60.09 m, with 1 foot / 39.48 cm to spare—a standard roll is 25 feet / 7.62 m long).

Twine

METHOD

1. Drill the posts into each corner of the garden bed so that each post is secure and vertical.

2. Starting with one post, wrap the outside perimeter of the bed with the chicken wire, attaching the wire at each corner tightly to the poles with twine. Leave the ends loosely fastened to the first post to permit the wire to open and close when accessing the bed.

3. Make sure to check the bottoms of the wire so there are no gaps that a small animal can sneak through.

BED ANNEXES

Another challenge I face with raised beds is that I can never predict exactly how much area a plant will cover. A few plants always fail to take, but others will fill in the spaces in the beds, and a couple will take off trailing out of and beyond the garden bed. I tame some, but others I want to grow to their full potential, particularly if they will bear fruit! When a plant is busting through, it needs support. In addition to cucumbers and zucchinis, I grow a number of Asian cucurbits: loofah, wax winter melon, bitter melon. I don't have to do a lot— they seem to grow pest-free, and the more humid, hot, and rainy the weather, the more they smile. I make an annex for these types of plants, especially the large winter melon when it takes off. The idea is to move the bed to suit the plant, not move the plant to suit the bed. I now have eight winter melons for the winter, much more than expected, and most of them growing on top of the annex. I just extend the growing area of the bed with a 2-foot / 60.96 cm raised fence and chicken wire on top so that the melon can grow off the side of the bed and suspended above the ground without restriction.

A-Frame Trellis

I was very excited to see my neighbors, the Hujiaks, produce hundreds of cucumbers out of one 5-foot-square trellis garden. They shared their bounty of cucumbers all summer long, and I made pickles four ways: hot and sour, smashed with sesame, Szechuan spicy, and a quick pickle in rice wine vinegar with a little sugar. I went back, got the specs for their homemade trellis, and made one this winter, forager-style.

This trellis is constructed in the shape of an A-frame with a horizontal pole suspended between two triangular frames. The Hujiaks made theirs with hinges at the top of the two frames so that they can fold it up for the winter. Mine is built to be permanently outdoors, so I have used sturdy, rot-resistant pitch pine.

When working with natural materials there is a lot of variability. The finished pieces have an irregular character and charm compared to straight precut lumber. There will be curves (even on the straightest pieces) and knotholes and different tones on the bark. The great thing about starting to work with wild wood is that you develop a whole new appreciation for the plant, more than you ever would just walking by it.

When using wild wood such as our young pitch pines, one end of the log will not be the same diameter as the other (sometimes markedly so). I balance the unevenness by joining a skinnier log to a wider log and drilling a screw into the skinnier log to ensure a secure attachment. In order for a screw to join two logs, it needs to be thin enough that the screw can go a fair amount into the next log.

This project is flexible. You can position each of the four "legs" of the trellis on the inner side of bricks, or stones, or drilled into the walls of

a garden bed. The chicken wire component can also be skipped, as in the photo, if you're looking for less structure.

• **The final measurements are 4 feet / 1.22 m long by 3 feet / .91 m wide, with 5-foot / 1.5 m diagonal-height end beams.** (*Note:* I am such a novice that I made this indoors in the dead of winter and forgot to check whether it would fit through the door to take it outside in the spring. Luckily, I could take it apart easily, removing the screws with a drill by pressing the reverse button.)

MATERIALS

5 pitch pine or other evergreen tree poles, 5 feet / 1.5 m tall (branches cut off), about 2 inches / 5.08 cm diameter, for the diagonal poles and top pole.

4 pitch pine poles, 4 feet / 1.22 m long, about 3 inches / 7.62 cm diameter, for bracing. Alternative option: use bricks, stone, or dig the poles into the dirt inside the raised bed.

Rubber bands or zip ties

10 outdoor deck screws, 3 inches / 7.62 cm

2 pieces **wire mesh**, 60 inches / 152.4 cm by 47 inches / 119.38 m (cattle or horse fencing, or chicken wire), cut in between the cells so that the long ends are available for wrapping.

Wire cutters, heavy duty

Optional: Heavy-duty electrician cable staples (if your wire and poles are thin enough to be held by these)

Heavy twine (I use undyed hemp or sisal)

METHOD

Assemble the wood frame.

1. Position two of the 5-foot / 1.52 m pine poles so they cross diagonally at the top, like a flat tepee.

2. Secure the cross by attaching a thick rubber band (or zip tie) to the poles at the juncture where they connect to each other.

3. Further secure by wrapping over with twine or cordage. My pine poles are very heavy; I can still carry them, but they are heavier than plywood or boards.

4. Add additional support by drilling through the center of the X with a deck screw.

5. Secure two more of the 5-foot / 1.52 m poles the same way. You now have two Xs of poles.

6. Build a brace of the four 4-foot / 1.22 m pitch pines and attach the legs of the two Xs to the brace using deck screws (see diagram).

I have used 12.5 gauge, which is very heavy wire mesh. You could certainly go lighter, but with 12.5 gauge, the structure is incredibly sturdy and well made, and it will last for years. Also, bending the cut ends of the wires around the pine poles was a solid way to fasten with the heavier gauge. For more on gauge choices, see page 28.

7. Attach the remaining 5-foot / 1.52 m pole running across the X frame.

Attach the wire.

1. Have one person hold the top of the first wire panel flush with the top horizontal pole of the trellis. The other person will wrap the left and right trailing ends of the wire panel by bending them around the pitch pine diagonal poles. This gauge wire is stiff and so the final wire panel will make a firm structure that is long-lasting.

2. Wrap twine creatively around screws and other joints as well as at intervals on the top horizontal pole to hold the wire in place.

3. Repeat on the other side of the frame.

There will be a gap between the bottom of the wire panel and the ground (the wire panel was 47 inches / 119.38 cm, and the trellis is about 60 inches / 152.4 cm tall).

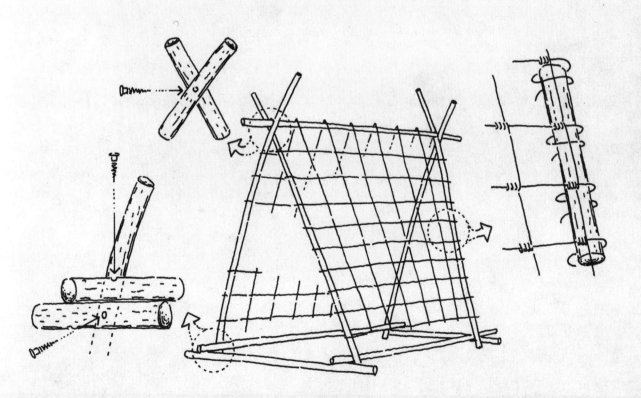

ON VINING

Some vines produce massive amounts of leafy material in the summer but die back in the winter. I need supports for them to clamber on, but I don't need these year-round. So I make a string trellis. Before considering the support for your vines, determine how the vines grow: by twining or tendril.

Twining vines: Wisteria and honeysuckle are often invasive and they can and do twine with no support, and would eventually strangle a support.

Tendril vines: The little tendrils of these vines come out from stems or at the base of leaves or leafstalks. Passionflower, peas, and grapes grow like this. These plants need some help to grow a certain way, or they may tendril over themselves. Twenty years ago I planted two passionflower seedlings I bought from a local nature center. Although a perennial, it dies back in the winter here in New Jersey and is slow to start in the spring. The first year I even thought New Jersey weather had killed it. But now I know better, and by June its tendrils are up, searching for something to climb.

Porch Vine Garland

To help my passionflower grow up over the columns on the porch, I run a string that they can coil around like a garland, forming a living frame in the summer. Since the passionflower dies back in the winter, I just cut the string to take it down and dry most of the vine for winter teas. I love the look of tea made with whole leaves and tendrils.

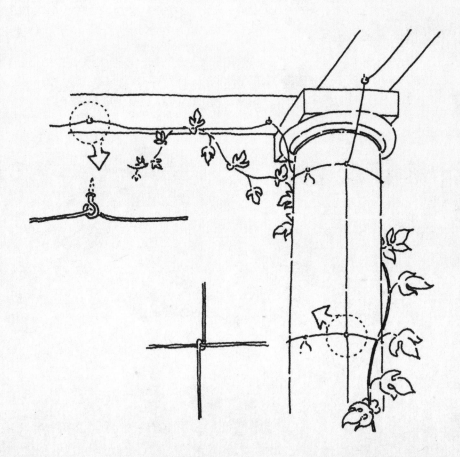

MATERIALS

Ladder to reach the porch eaves

4 outdoor steel screw eyehooks

Ball of string or twine

Passionflower or other tendril vine (trumpet vine, grape)

METHOD

1. Screw the hooks into the top inner eave of the porch approximately 24 inches / 60.96 cm apart, starting at the corner where the vertical post or column meets the eave.

2. Wrap the end of the ball of string around the base of the column and tie a knot.

3. Unravel the ball end upward 24 inches / 60.96 cm, loop it around the column, and make a half knot where the ends meet. Pull tight but with a slight give so that the vine can get its tendrils under and around the string and column.

4. Unravel the ball end another 24 inches / 60.96 cm up and repeat, looping around the column, making a half knot, and then extending up again.

5. When you reach the top of the column, thread the string through the eyehooks and continue the same method on the other column.

6. Tie the last loop around the base of the other column and secure with a full knot. Cut the end.

7. As the passionflower vine grows, gently guide the tendrils under the string. They will happily accommodate.

CHAPTER SEVEN

STEWARD-SHIP

ON TENDING PLANTS 143

THE ART OF WEEDING (SELECTIVELY) 145

PLANT LIFE CYCLES 148

PLANT GROWTH HABITS 149

FIELD TIPS FOR MANAGING INVASIVE PLANTS 150

Ⓡ   Japanese Knotweed Pickle and Soda 155

Ⓟ   Deer Fence 156

On Tending Plants

When I first started out, squeezing through subway turnstiles and lugging bags of wild nettle into restaurants, the front-of-house staff at a well-known restaurant asked me to come talk to them about what I do. Farmers, fishmongers, artisan beekeepers all love to explain their passion so that the staff can translate this provenance from land or sea to the diner's plate. The manager introduces me: "Hi, everyone. This is Tama. She has come down from the mountain to talk about her great products." Silly me. I hadn't thought to call what I was bringing products (and hey, do they really think there are mountains in New Jersey?). So I started off by saying sheepishly that these aren't my products because I didn't make them. Blank stares. Confusion.

What I really meant was that they aren't mine, I didn't make the plants—I just make room for them. Humans are stewards, not masters of the earth... As Pope Francis said in his 2015 encyclical *Laudato Si'*, "We are not God. The earth was here before us...to till and to keep." Buddhists say that our progeny are not our own creations, nor do we choose them. Instead, they choose us. We are blessed to be chosen as their innkeepers, but we are not their masters. We provide the nourishment, shelter, love, care, a little direction perhaps, but we do not own them. At some point they will leave the inn and continue on their own journey, perhaps returning from time to time. We do not control them according to our desires.

In the same way, stewards of the land serve as innkeepers for the plants that come to live in the garden. Some plants are already there, some move in, and others we plant. We provide a kind of framework and support; we help maintain the peace when they get ornery, try to dominate, or crowd out others. We don't lock them up in rooms that we set for them. We enjoy living alongside each other, seeing them grow. At some point we shall part ways, inevitably.

Stewardship and sustainability are not just inspirational words; it requires skill to observe, balance, and manage the plants in our care. Instead of reformulating everything and moving trees around from here to there, I leave the plants in the places they choose to grow, free-range, to self-breed, and I edit some of the more aggressive introduced plants to maintain diversity. Because, acknowledging change and time, the goal will not be a trophy but rather a constant tweaking; don't think of weeding as maintenance but rather as adaptation. These labors of stewardship are tedious, but the process of stewardship itself is rewarding. The process of weeding is the goal, because it is how I get to know plants.

THE ART OF WEEDING (SELECTIVELY)

I choke whenever I read articles about The Top Weeds to Get Rid Of because invariably most of them are my top plants too—to keep! Purslane, lambsquarters, and most of my Top Foraging Plants (page 76) are not only easy to grow, they also have more nutrients than most vegetables. My face lights up when I see them, and I am actively propagating them at my place because we can never seem to get enough. While my land thrives with indigenous plants, I do not aim to eradicate all others. Nonnative, so-called adventitious plants, especially when utilized for food and other purposes, have a place here as well, so long as they are not invasive and do not overwhelm others. Besides, virtually all cultivated vegetables and farm crops are comprised of nonnative species, so there is a place for both.

My focus is not "weeding," per se, but I admit that some weeds are not my favorites, such as thistle, which has edible roots but is too much trouble and not so delicious, despite the fact that the Japanese like to pickle the one-year-old roots (how can I tell if it's one or two years old??). Or ground ivy: yes, I do forage it, and it can pair nicely in an infusion or in chocolate brownies, but only in the early part of the spring when it is flowering, and it can drown out other voices in the garden; or stilt grass and other invasives… But I don't like to say I am weeding, because that implies an indiscriminate yank with a hoe. I think of it more as editing, which lets the plants be but makes more room for the other weeds.

To edit, I peer closely at shoots emerging as if they are part of a miniature bonsai garden. In one three-by-six-foot bed there might be twenty or more new plants to be curious about. I edit out invasives before they get a hold (even one mugwort plant or a lesser celandine is a brewing problem) and leave space for new emergent plants to spread out.

I don't pull out small shoots as they emerge from the soil, whether garden or flowerpot.

Knowing what baby plants will become is a great skill for foragers, gardeners, and farmers—to know plants as they grow, not just when flowering. When the first two leaves (cotyledons) break through the ground they may not look anything like the true leaves of the plant. Wait until at least the true leaves form. In this way over the years I have learned what they grow into and now can recognize seedlings when they're only one inch high.

Scott Bernstein, my friend Marcia's husband, practices tough love weeding: anything that doesn't look like a planted bush he hoes away. Over the years many indigenous and other plants Marcia wanted to enjoy have gone away with the hoe. Lena Struwe, a friend and botany professor, recommends a scientific data approach to resolve the ongoing disputes between spouses: first take a photo of the emerging plant with a blank label or stick next to it. Continue to take photos over the next few weeks, recording the plant growth and what it became. Note the date, write on the label what the plant is, and the next year, you are set.

Any given area or garden bed may harbor the same weeds year after year, because weed seeds can stay viable in the soil for decades. And there can be a lot of them. So, while I have a lot of ground ivy in my backyard, I have zero pineapple weed. My neighbor has a lot of pineapple weed and *Galinsoga* as well. You will get to know which are the same weeds you see over and over again and won't have to give a thought to looking them up after a while. As you can see from the "Knowing Plants" chapter, most of my Top Foraging Plants are weedy. I never weed out chickweed or purslane or lambsquarters. And I'm hoping to get more *Galinsoga*. These are low-growing plants, so they don't overshadow my herbs and vegetables. Rather, they keep the ground underneath moist and shady. If I pull out all the weeds in a bed, the soil quickly dries up and looks cakey, whereas the soil under the chickweed is soft and loamy.

I often hear from energetic people who are tackling tough invasive plants they find in the yard. They jump right in pulling, cutting, burning, spraying. But wait a minute. In order for a plan of attack to be effective, first learn how the plant grows and why it is so effective at spreading. Manage the garden based on this knowledge, or all efforts could be in vain or, worse, spread the plant further. (Conversely, if there is a native plant or other culinary plant that you wish to propagate, knowing its life cycle and means of growth are important to those efforts as well (see chapter eight, "Making More Plants," page 160).

PLANT
LIFE CYCLES

Annuals: Complete their life cycle every year; i.e., annually. This is the typical gardening cycle: buy new seed every year in spring, plant, tend, let die, plant again the next year. Most vegetable plants other than heirloom seeds are annuals, as are potted nursery plants like pansies. I never understood why someone would want to keep buying and replanting the same plants year after year. Some of these plants are bred to be sterile and will not even set seed.

Annual wild plants can germinate every year from seed, sometimes more than once a year. They set profusions of seed that can last for years in the ground until conditions (open ground, climate, light) are right to germinate. Some of these have been so successful at seeding that they outcompete other plants, and are not just weedy but invasive.

Winter annuals are plants that set seed at the end of the summer, overwinter, and then set seeds in early spring before dying. Plants that you may think of as early-spring plants are up so early because they never died out in the winter, they were just semidormant or static; for example, garlic pennycress (*Thlaspi alliaceum* or *T. arvense*).

Biannuals: Plants with a life cycle of two years. The first year they will not flower. The second year they flower and seed. In the spring they seed and germinate, and over the winter they form a basal rosette low to the ground. Usually, flavor is very concentrated in these plants, without much sugar, so they are on the bitter end of the spectrum. If I don't want them to spread, I cut them before they set seed. For example, carrots and beets are biannuals, but they are harvested the first year and not left in the ground to flower and run to seed. Many umbellifer plants (dill, fennel, Queen Anne's lace) are biannuals.

Perennials: Some perennials return the next year, but many are short-lived. An example is dandelion. It forms a taproot and has a rosette, and the next year (spring to summer) it flowers and sets seed. Then you see it again overwintering as a dormant (and once in a while flowering) rosette. This rosette can be tough and bitter as it ages.

Other perennials are longer lived. Trees, shrubs, and vines fall into this category, but many herbs and plants do as well. Some of these perennials spread vigorously through rapid growth, above as well as underground, in addition to producing seed. Trying to kill off mugwort or tree of heaven, for example, by merely cutting them before they seed would be futile.

Depending on the climate and situation, plants that are biannuals in one place can act as annuals or even perennials in another place. And they can end up being annuals if we treat them as such (like digging out the roots of beets and turnips). These categories are helpful but not unbreakable.

PLANT GROWTH HABITS

Nodes: The node is the center of growth for a plant. A node can be located on a stem or a branch or a root. The node area is where new buds will develop for stems, flowers, or leaves. For any twig or leaf, the place where it attaches to the stem is the node. The nodes in some plants can also look like joints or ringed sections dividing up the stems (see illustration, page 154).

Rhizomes: Plant stems can grow extensively underground via rhizomes. It is a good survival technique for plants, because if conditions aboveground are unfavorable, they can persist underground and find new territory. It is easy to overlook how far the rhizome may have spread since it is hidden from plain sight. Furthermore, if a piece of rhizome with a node breaks off, it can form a new plant if it finds itself in favorable conditions. In this way, a heavy rain or flood can spread even small rhizomes all along the flood zone.

Suckers: These are growths of aboveground shoots that may arise from nodal points on rhizomes or from a tree stem or root. If a plant is pruned, the action may cause the plant to invigorate, to grow more thickly, to send out new shoots/suckers during the growing season. Hazelnuts and sumac are examples. I have noticed that the original "mama" tree tends to weaken and die out as the new suckers shoot up.

FIELD TIPS FOR MANAGING INVASIVE PLANTS

Invasive plants (noxious weeds as opposed to just plain old weeds) are so successful in their spread that they crowd out other plants and upset the species diversity and ecological balance of a place, so they need additional attention to keep them in line. These plants were often introduced by humans, and unlike many common weeds, they do not necessarily depend on continued disturbance of the ground by humans. Once they gain a foothold, invasive plants will persist in natural areas such as forests and meadows. Whereas I may see weeds such as garlic pennycress (yum!) spreading like wannabe invaders in my garden bed, these weeds do not spread into the meadow, forest, or along the creek. Almost every area of the world now has its version of invasive plants, which thrive in a new place without their usual, natural checks and balances (insects, disease, climate). Canada goldenrod is invasive in China. Japanese knotweed, *Reynoutria japonica* or *Fallopia japonica*, is invasive in the United States and beyond. Start with knowing the plants, their seasonal timings, method(s) of perpetuation, and so on in order to exert some effective management over them.

Invasive applies to all species, not just plants, that are "non-native to the ecosystem and whose introduction causes or is likely to cause economic or environmental harm or harm to human health" (Executive Order 13112 - Invasive Species, (1999)). For resources on learning the invasive species in your state, start with invasive.org.

For heavy infestations, I have had some success with long-term solarization: using the heat of the sun to control pests and weeds by covering the soil so that the sun's heat over an extended period of time bakes and kills off visible weeds (see method on page 152 and illustration at right for controlling mugwort).

Although professionals will often need to resort to strong herbicidal controls, this requires licensing, and since I am eating many of these same weeds, I avoid introducing heavy chemical treatments. Even with herbicides, I have seen populations on other properties resprout after, say, three years (mugwort, knotweed, and garlic mustard are examples). This may be because the traffic on the site (whether through wildlife or humans) is such that it continues to bring seed from nearby sites, or because the plant is only nine-tenths killed off, and the one-tenth regenerates over time. Local universities and plant societies can advise you, as methods may differ for different sites and conditions. It is more realistic to approach managing invasives realizing that it requires vigilant stewardship rather than thinking you can spray them one year and then forget about it. And remember to determine the plant's life cycle and mode of growth to avoid wasting time on futile or even invigorating methods!

HERBACEOUS RHIZOMATOUS PLANTS

There has been some misinformation about invasive plants; for example, that they can spread simply from a piece of leaf (incorrect unless using tissue culture). That is why it is important to understand the growth habit of the plant—whether you are trying to encourage it or discourage it. To contain a plant that spreads by rhizome, do not burn, pull, tug, or cut at the base, as this will encourage new robust growth underground.

Mugwort *(Artemisia vulgaris)* is another beloved Asian plant with both culinary and medicinal properties. In Korea you can visit a mugwort well-being spa. A poem from Japan: "Search I must for a way to visit you, dwelling so long with the grasses and yomogi [mugwort] on an unbeaten track" *(Tale of the Genji)*. In spring: "in between the withered clumps are seen the fresh green of yomogi" (Hatsuko. In *Chado: The Way of Tea*. Tuttle, 2005).

Solarization:

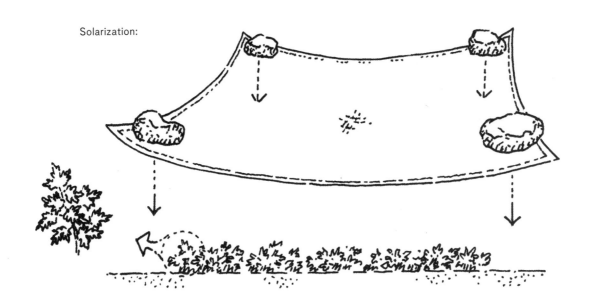

Mugwort leaves look like chrysanthemum, with silvery undersides. Unlike chrysanthemum, it spreads extensively by rhizome and its flowers produce a high amount of pollen, which is extremely allergy-inducing.

CONTROL METHODS

Solarization: I have been able to control mugwort on a preserve by covering with a heavy plastic tarp. It cannot be a loose cloth or a small roll because the mugwort is so robust it will push up the fabric and thrive underneath. When I tried this, we left it on for a year and the mugwort has not regenerated so far.

Removing: Attack while young, emerging. In small areas, if I spy even one little mugwort plant in a garden bed, I pull it out, making sure that my hands follow the rhizome underground, and I tug so that it does not break off in the ground. A small amount of rhizome can generate a new plant, and pulling or cutting without removing the entire rhizome may invigorate the plant into a growth spurt during growing season.

Mowing: Mow very, very low when it reaches about six inches, but before it flowers.

Harvesting: Cut, dry, eat, and repeat. Mugwort is delicious in soup or tempura-fried, or when mature, can be dried and used as an aromatic in a smudge stick.

Shading: Shade it out. Mugwort does not favor shaded areas.

WOODY RHIZOMATOUS PLANTS

Decapitation followed by bud-picking: We have had some limited success with what we term the decapitation method for tall plants and trees. To use the decapitation method, cut between knee-high and waist-high so that the plant tries to regrow only at the top of the stump. We cut at the internode, not at a node where it is primed to regrow. (We tested Japanese knotweed and it did start to grow from the joint node.) If you cut it to the ground, or just tug at the rhizome, it will grow back bushier and thicker. With *Aralia elata*, Japanese (Korean-Chinese) Angelica tree, we harvest the leaf buds, a delicacy in East Asia, by sawing off the tree waist high when the leaves are budding (and keeping the buds); because the tree is still tall enough, it does not send out suckers. The next year it will try to leaf out from these lopped areas, and if we pick off those buds as well, it becomes significantly weakened. In its native habitat in Japan, the aralia tree looks delicate and graceful. Japanese foraging notes warn to be careful not to pick *all* the buds as it will eventually kill the tree. But where it forms invasive colonies in the United States, it is far more robust and tall than the photos show in Japan, so this could be a worthy goal.

I'm always looking for ways that I can better serve the land as a steward, by harvesting these invasives to use in place of wood or cord, for wellness, and especially as food. I often go back to where the plant originated and see if the culture there uses it, so I have foraging books from different regions of the world. I respect these traditions, but most of the time I need to change them to suit my own needs, since the plant itself is a product of time and *terroir* and sometimes behaves differently as it adapts to a land thousands of miles away.

BAMBOO

Many years ago an elderly neighbor of ours called 911: "Help me—the bamboo my husband planted; he passed away and now the bamboo is moving in, surrounding the house."

It turns out her husband was an illustrator and planted the bamboo as a screen hedge and also planted different species so he could draw them and incorporate them in the books he worked on. After identifying them, as many types are not edible and even more are not delicious, we saw most were *Phyllostachys angusta, stone bamboo,* and *P. atrovaginata,* incense bamboo. These are running bamboos that spread vigorously by underground rhizomes. My activities don't eradicate but do help control the spread by snapping off the outermost shoots from an existing grove. Needless to say, we never plant this invasive and it is nowhere in my garden, except as dead wood for posts and fencing stakes.

In the spring, when the shoots are six to ten inches high, I snap off the shoots and bring them home to sauté with beef and chili sauce, to slice with ground pork and ginger, to pickle, to stew with coconut milk and chicken. The season is so short that I try to eat it as many ways as possible. My favorite is homemade hot-and-sour soup with real, fresh, "gone wild" bamboo shoots.

Peel off the outer layers to reveal the inner pale yellow core. Cut in chunks or slice. These so-called "winter" shoots are tender and sweet, so you don't need to boil for an hour to reduce bitterness, as is the case with the more bitter giant bamboo. Other species of bamboo have an acrid or bitter aftertaste and carry toxins that need to be boiled in order to be edible.

VINES

Japanese honeysuckle (*Lonicera japonica*) is a prolific vine, beautiful but sadly one of the top invasive plants in the United States. The vine is beloved in Asia for its heady scent, medicinal properties, and flowers of two colors (separate white and yellow flowers on the same plant); in Chinese it is *jinyinhua* (gold-silver flower), in Japanese *tsuitsui* (sucking flower). You can pick it and suck the golden honey-like liquid dripping off the flower stem. This plant was intentionally introduced ornamentally and for erosion control in the United States. It is a tenacious, woody, perennial semi-evergreen vine that can spread vegetatively along the forest floor and into fields and meadows. It grows up onto small shrubs and trees, seeking more light to flower and fruit, wrapping and squeezing so tightly that I can see the marks in the trunk of the tree, maimed so that the trunk looks like a corkscrew. The tree will perish unless I unwrap the tight vine coils where they are pinching the tree. On hands and knees, I tug it out where it emerges from the earth and follow the entire runners across the open forest floor.

When I don't have time to pull out the vine, I at least cut it away near the ground so that the top mass dies back and frees the trees. This method is often referred to as the "window" treatment. Cut the vine at shoulder height with garden clippers and again around the bottom of the tree where the vine emerges from the ground.

When I gather a large amount of blooming honeysuckle, I use the flowers for tea (page 206), and leafy vines for wattle and fence structures. Eddy Leroux, Executive Chef of Restaurant DANIEL, plucks the flowers off the vine at peak aroma and infuses them in a mixed mild oil, such as grapeseed and canola. Leave at room temperature for three days, then refrigerate and drizzle over summer dishes.

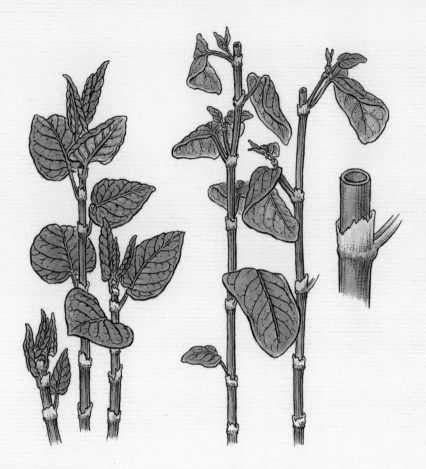

Japanese Knotweed

When I first started cutting knotweed, I looked for the most tender shoots. Knotweed is a woody plant and needs to be picked before it becomes too fibrous. Over time and after seeing thousands of knotweed patches, I realized that picking only the young plants can lead you in the wrong direction. Very mature patches, with large clumps of rhizomes, take longer to emerge in the spring, and when they do the shoots are fatter, juicier, and more tender (by tender I mean they are bendable). They can grow several feet before they become woody, whereas some small, less-mature patches are perhaps more ripe for eradication and not as good for eating.

Find a mature stand. Cut where the plant is still pliable and cut cleanly with sharp clippers. Do not cut the plant at a node (joint). Transport the top parts in a bag to your kitchen and do not drop pieces of nodes on the ground. The shoots will be hollow, so when you slice them crosswise, they look like pretty little rings. The knife will cut through tender shoots like butter. If you notice resistance, these shoots are already becoming woody and should be discarded. Knotweed is harvested wild in Japan and eaten in a *nabe* or boiled like asparagus and served with a dressing. Dried knotweed root is also used in traditional Chinese medicine to make tea as it is high in resveratrol, a natural antioxidant.

JAPANESE KNOTWEED PICKLE AND SODA

from Chef Nate Kuester of Naro, NYC

INGREDIENTS

1⅓ pounds / 600 g Japanese knotweed
(2–3 shoots, each 12 inches / 30.48 cm long),
sliced crosswise in sections 1 inch / 2.54 cm long

3 cups / 710 g water

3 cups / 600 g sugar

1 heaping tablespoon dried jasmine tea leaves

½ cup / 230 g lemon juice

METHOD

1. Place the sliced knotweed rings in a quart-size glass mason jar.

2. In a pot, heat the sugar and water until sugar is dissolved.

3. Infuse with the tea leaves for up to 4 minutes, then strain and pour over the knotweed rings.

4. Add the lemon juice.

5. Let cool and sit in a dark cool place for 2 days. Refrigerate.

Knotweed pickles are great with fish, on hamburgers, anywhere you use pickles. They give a refreshing acidity with some sweetness.

The beautiful rose-colored syrup that is left after the pickles are gone can be used as a basis for a tart knotweed soda. Mix one part syrup to four parts chilled tonic water. Garnish with mint.

Deer Fence

The white-tailed deer is a wild species, indigenous to North America, but its lack of predation and adaptability to living near humans have led to a population explosion. Their increased presence, in addition to contributing to a number of automobile accidents, throws a wrench in plant diversity and regeneration of forests; the deer graze heavily on saplings as well as herbaceous native plants (although in the last five years we have observed they have developed a taste for knotweed tips). Deer can eat two thousand pounds of greens a year, and when deer are hungry, they will eat almost anything, which is why plants are labeled "deer resistant" but not "deer proof." Deer can jump over fences six feet high and crawl under small gaps, so building a sturdy fence to keep deer out (and pets or children in) is essential, but can be prohibitive in cost and labor. As a stopgap or for a smaller area, use the chicken wire cages on page 28. However, we deer-fenced our meadow and surrounding area (about five acres) with only one youngish thirty-year-old, about five foot eleven inches tall, to help. I needed the fence to be sturdy to hold up against the weight of a deer bashing against it to get in, but also self-repairable when the inevitable tree or storm (two major hurricanes!) damaged it.

Metal wire is key to sturdy, sustainable fencing, with deer fencing requiring the most sturdy wire. The best material to use will depend on the purpose of the fence. Consider:

1. **Strength:** For fencing, the wire gauge (ga.) is the key determinant to look at, as this indicates the thickness of the wire; i.e., its strength. Gauge runs from 9 (the strongest; will keep in an angry bull, some say) to 16 (weakest); so remember, in this case, the higher the gauge number, the weaker and lighter the wire. (The gauge numbers are based on how many times the metal has to run

through some doohickey machine; the thinner and lighter the wire is, the more times it can wrap through.) For a deer fence, use 14 gauge. You will often see these called cattle, hog, or horse fences; they are strong enough to keep out larger animals. For smaller critters or pets, use 16 gauge or chicken wire.

2. **Height:** Deer can jump a fence 6 feet / 1.83 m high, depending on what's around it.

3. **Weight:** None of the online advice I read mentioned weight, but this is a serious and practical consideration if you don't plan on hiring a crew. Stronger doesn't always mean better, because the stronger the wire, the more it weighs. The wire is sold in rolls, so there will be a minimum weight per roll. To give you an idea, I cannot even lift the side of a roll of 12.5-gauge cattle fence 47 inches / 121.92 cm high (weighs around 150 lb. / 68 kg). Although 12.5-gauge wire would certainly keep deer out, you would need to get a tractor or other vehicle plus crew to haul the stuff around—not to mention lifting it and stretching it around the super-strong posts you'd need. For this reason, I suggest 14-gauge wire for a deer fence. • **This project will yield 50 feet / 15.24 m of fencing.**

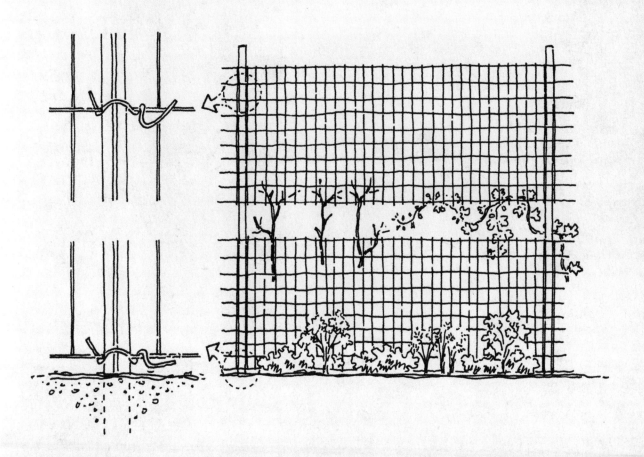

1 metal post (sometimes referred to as T-posts) for every 6–8 feet / 1.82–2.43 m of fencing, minimum 8 feet / 2.43 m in height. Substitute trees for posts if the fence will run along a tree line.

Metal fence post driver (3 inches / 7.62 cm diameter, 24 inches / 60.96 cm long by 6 inches / 15.24 cm wide (includes handles)

1 roll 14-gauge **welded wire fencing**, 2 by 4-inch / 5.08 by 10.16 cm mesh, 36 inches / 91.44 cm high (instead of 47 inches / 121.92 cm high, so each roll is light enough for one person to lug around without a problem using a wheelbarrow)

Steel T-post fence clips, 4 per post

T-post clip bender tool (can buy cheaply, look for "clip bender"). Put the clip in the hole in the clip bender and bend it up like a lever. You can also use pliers, but it takes longer.

Rolls of **welded wire fencing** come in standard lengths of 100 feet / 30.48 m, so one roll will make 2 lengths, enough for one 50-foot / 15.24 m fence.

METHOD

1. First walk the area you want to fence off.

2. Install posts 6–8 feet / 1.82–2.43 m apart. Position the metal fence post driver over the top of the pole (if you are too short, you have to place the pole on the ground horizontally and then right the pole). Bang the post driver up and down on the top of the pole, hammering the pole into the ground. The pole needs to go into the ground at least 12 inches / 30.48 cm.

3. Next, attach the first roll of cattle wire to each pole on the bottom 4 feet / 1.22 m of the pole using the T-post clips to fasten the wire to the pole.

4. Attach the second upper roll, leaving a 12-inch / 30.48 cm gap in between the top of the first roll and the bottom of the second roll, so that the very top edge is 7 feet / 2.13 m off the ground The fence has to be tight so that it doesn't sag in the middle, making it easy for a deer to push or bend down. I like to find one side where there is a very strong tree or post and attach the fence to that. Then we attach it to another pole 6–8 feet / 1.82–2.43 m away. (This is another reason it helps that the roll is not one giant roll 10 feet / 3 m high, because it would need a lot of strength and possibly a winch to stretch the roll tight enough, given its volume and weight.) If you note any gapping areas, pop another pole in between.

Now the upcycling part: to make room for us to pound in the fence poles and hang the rolls of fencing, we had to cut away some shrubs (invasives such as autumn olive, multiflora rose) and cut back branches of trees (pin oak, pine). What to do with these piles when the compost bin is already brimming over? Ah! Weave the brush into the gaps between the fencing in order to strengthen it and provide a more visible mesh barrier. First, we use cut branches as woody structure that we stand upright or diagonally top to bottom, weaving once or twice vertically across both wire panels. This is a great use for winter pruning debris.

Next—and in late fall or early spring it is easier to do—we cut younger shoots of shrubs and weave them into the gap in the rolls of wire. The long green shoots can be twisted among the wire and will harden as they dry.

Finally, we use invasive vines such as honeysuckle almost like twine to further tie up the fence. We love using the innate strength of "trash" invasive plants to support our fence! We do this on days when the weather is pleasant, and at different times of the year for a few hours— not all at once.

Aside from the fact that the work goes fast, the weaving motion with hand, mind, and eye, feeling the plant, its texture and pliability as we twist it into the wire, is enjoyable and creative work. In some ways it is like making a natural espalier.

Note: The autumn olive and shrubs do grow back, since I am not using herbicide on them, but I just keep on using them; it's a cycle: grow back, cut, weave into fence, repeat next year.

CHAPTER EIGHT

Making MORE PLANTS

SINGULAR PLANTS OF A TIME AND PLACE 163

COLLECTING SEEDS 165

 Collecting Wild Seeds in the Field 166

STORING SEEDS 168

SOWING SEEDS 168

TAKING CUTTINGS 169

Ⓡ Lemon Basil and Wild Lemon Balm Pesto 170

TRANSPLANTING WHOLE PLANTS 173

Ⓐ Trench Planting 175

Ⓡ Longevity Spinach 178

Ⓡ Lime Leaf, Galangal, and Lemongrass Meatballs 179

Ⓐ Grow Lights 180

PLANT RESCUE 181

SINGULAR PLANTS OF A TIME AND PLACE

Life begins inside a seed. The DNA for the future comes packaged in receptacles of all shapes and sizes; the tiniest speck can contain the secrets of the next generation. And yet, as plants struggle from habitat decline, extreme weather, and invasive species, I have come to believe that saving seeds is one of the most fulfilling things I can do. When I save and sow seeds, I always carry hope that some will bear fruit in the future, even if I am not there to see it. And I think this hidden hope for something more lasting is shared: sown separately, enjoyed collectively.

The **Let Standing method**: Push aside any brush remaining on the ground around the plants as they begin to form seed; simply let them hang over open ground and they will reseed themselves. Most herbaceous annual or biannual weedy species do just fine this way.

Wild plants may produce seed in spring, summer, fall, and in between. With seed, timing is critical, although not easily marked on a calendar. Not all these seeds will ripen, and not all ripe seeds will produce new plants. Many of the genetics of seed evolution are still unknown.

Each plant may operate on its own rhythm; within one species some are early seeders, some are late seeders. All this individualism, rather than being a drag on planning, builds resiliency. Seasonal weather is increasingly unreliable; instead of April showers, we could get April snow, April drought, or an April heat wave. During a sudden hot spell in the spring, over the course of only forty-eight hours, the *Cardamine hirsuta* upland cress stems shot up tall and lanky, the leaves shrank to little flippers; the plants rapidly flowered and propelled seed to the ground in the unusual warmth. The world is becoming more complicated as the plants navigate fickleness.

By tending certain plants to form plant communities of a time and place, you can steward the land toward resilience and genetic diversity. One species of *Passiflora incarnata* in Georgia will have DNA variation from one in New Jersey, though both carry the same name. This is why it is more meaningful to nurture plants that sprang from your own ground, rather than raze everything and install plants from somewhere else. A restoration ecologist, Dr. Gerould Wilhelm, told me that the test of a successful restoration is that the wild native plants produce progeny; they begin to breed on their own, establishing their own communities and populations. These are the singular plants, adapted to the terroir of Your Township in the late years of the Anthropocene era.

So how to start? The easiest and time-honored way is the **Let Standing method** of the Middle Ground. Let nature dance away.

COLLECTING SEEDS

Plants cannot move. So, in order to ensure a wider dispersal of their progeny, greater diversity, and increased survival, they get around these shortcomings by various means such as a) floating away in the wind or water, b) storing the seed in a juicy fruit that is carried to a new place by birds and other foraging animals or insects such as ants, c) hitching a ride by attaching little burrs and other stick 'ems to the outside of the seed coat to be carried by humans and wildlife, or d) ballistically dispersing the seed by their own mechanical catapult. Some examples of plants with explosive seeds are jewelweed, yellow wood sorrel, and upland cress (*Cardamine hirsuta*). When collecting seeds in the field, exercise caution and ensure that you don't carry some unwanted progeny back with you in the form of seeds. High rubber boots help.

Do not dig up a fancy wildflower in the field and transport it home. For a better chance that the species will live and a better way to respect the ecology of the wild, collect seed using the following field protocols I learned from the MidAtlantic Seed Bank and Greenbelt Native Nursery (scaled wayyyy down).

These protocols apply to native herbaceous plants, both cultivated and wild; trees and woody plants deserve a whole different regimen of specific techniques and have larger space requirements. I also do not collect seeds of invasive plants. Where I have a population of potentially or emerging invasive plants such as shiso or wild fennel, I am careful to confine them to the garden bed area.

Collecting Wild Seeds in the Field

As in any good foraging, you first need to determine the size of the local population. Observe how the plant is scattered through the landscape. Is it clustered in wetter areas? A spot here or there? In a mass? Make sure not to miss the outliers, on the fringe. Heather Liljengren, field botanist and seed collector for New York City's Department of Parks & Recreation Greenbelt Native Plant Center (GNPC), reminds me that the plants living on the edge may be the most important for preserving genetic diversity.

What you need:

- paper bags
- clippers
- a permanent ink pen
- a field notebook or clipboard with seed collection form
- Permission from the property owner. Public parks do not permit collecting seeds.

1. Once you have determined that there is a healthy population, gather seed but do not collect more than 20 percent of the seed from a given native plant species.

2. Collect seed from multiple plants, ideally from thirty to fifty different plants of the same species.

3. Collect seed on different days, if possible. Seed does not all ripen at the same time, and this way your seed collection will include both early-seeding and later-seeding plants.

4. The seed needs to be ripe! BEFORE CUTTING, pry open one of the seedpods. The seed itself should be hard and not be able to be split with your thumbnail. Although color alone is not an indicator, many ripe seeds have turned from green to brown or gray. The seeds should be whole and not be shattered or moldy. Other indicators of ripeness are that the pod has split open and that the seeds are about to spill out.

5. Cut the entire seedpod into a paper bag. Label it immediately.

HOW TO HARVEST EXPLOSIVE SEEDS

Prepare a piece of cardboard or stiff paper about 8 by 11 inches / 20 by 28 cm by layering with overlapping painter's masking tape, sticky-side up.

Cut the top of the plant when the seedpods have formed. Select a flat outdoor surface, sheltered from the wind. Carefully lay the plant over the top of the tape and touch the seedpod. They will explode and, although some seeds will miss the tape, a majority should be captured.

Gently soak the tape in a bowl of water to dissolve the glue and free the seeds. Drain off the water carefully so as not to disturb the seed. Lay the seeds out on a paper towel to dry and store.

STORING SEEDS

SOWING SEEDS

Generally, once seed is dry to the touch, it can be stored in paper envelopes. Label and file the envelopes in an airtight container to keep out rodents or insects. Stored in a cool place (40–55°F / 4.4–12.8°C) with low humidity, and without direct sunlight, many seeds can be viable for years.

Where: Expert propagators of wild plants always chat with me about where I have seen plants growing in the wild as a clue to what type of landscape the plant will favor beyond basic internet information. When I see sumac clustering on banks sloping down to the highway, it's not difficult to fathom that sumac likes full sun, on dry slopy south-facing edges without a lot of competition from larger trees.

When: Although spring is indeed the season of planting for many cultivated crops, wild plants often follow a different rhythm. Their best time to plant is often the time just before the winter or off-season. Wild plants in temperate zones have adapted to a cold period, and the seeds often develop a hard outer coat, so they will not germinate until after a period of winter-like conditions. Seed collectors can try to mimic nature and this cold period or other conditions required to jump-start germination. I have had some success propagating from seed with more hardy and weedier species, but I have the most success when I don't try to mimic nature, I just give the seeds back to nature and scatter them.

Do not scatter seed on a windy day (common sense). Do time the planting to the day or even the hour before a period of gentle rain. Do not plant right after a heavy storm or any other time when there is standing water. Waterlogged soils mean that the water sits in the porous soils where there would normally be air. Plants need oxygen in the soil to grow. Conversely, if there is a drought, the seeds may lie dormant for a considerable time until conditions are more favorable. I do not water sown seed on a larger landscape; it may "tease" plants to germinate and grow when it is not the right natural condition for them to thrive.

How: The seeds need to have contact with soil. If there is a thick cover of grass or other plant life, the ground can be scratched up lightly about ½ inch / 13 mm deep so that the top mat of organic matter is cast aside and the soil peeks through. Scratching is not as deep as tilling, which usually goes down 8–10 inches / 20–25 cm. This level of deeper disturbance breaks up the mycorrhizal associations in the soil, releases carbon, and exposes "weed" seeds, unselected, to the light.

My default method for eliminating cover plants, especially for thick matted grass or a strongly rooted plant such as dock, is to solarize with a tarp (see page 152).

How to broadcast seed across a larger area: On open ground larger than a raised bed, I hand-broadcast seed. Native seeds are often small and light, and many standard crop seeders are not calibrated appropriately. Buy fine sand and mix the sand with the seed in a ratio of five to one in a bucket. Walk the area and cast the seed in an arc. The sand helps to keep the seed from blowing away and also marks the area so that you can avoid retracing your steps and also fill in any bare spots.

After sowing: Have patience. Go away and exercise some benign neglect, only checking in to edit out any lurking invasive plants.

TAKING CUTTINGS

Cuttings begin with an existing plant and make new plants out of them. So, unlike seeds, the new plant does not expand the genetic diversity of a species, but these vegetative clones are an inexpensive and easy way to propagate herbaceous plants and even extend their growing season. I also discovered during the pandemic that I couldn't always rely on nurseries to have what I wanted in stock.

UPRIGHT STEMS: ABOVEGROUND

When: The best time to do this is during the growing season, from a mature healthy plant.

How: Remember to cut below the nodes, the points of growth for the plant, visible at the base of the leaf or bud where it joins the stem. If there are no leaves, there may be a small knob or a ring (such as a bamboo joint); a cutting to make a new plant needs to include at least one node, which will develop new growth, independent of the parent.

With some clean, sharp shears, make a stem cutting below the node. Trim off any large top leaves, in order to leave less stress for the plant, as well as any lower leaves that will end up underwater. Immediately place the cut stems in unchlorinated water in an open, clear glass bottle. Leave the jar on a sunny windowsill so you can see exactly the stages of root growth (as opposed to wondering what is happening belowground, if the cutting was placed directly in soil). Replace the water from time to time. When the roots have grown out to a fibrous mass, remove from the water and plant deeply in a pot with a mixture of potting and garden soil. The roots of these herbaceous stem plants, similar to tomato plants, should be buried deeply, because they will continue to grow roots from the stem after being planted in soil, creating a bushier and more robust root system. Water and press down lightly on the soil.

Herbaceous plants that are easy to grow from stem cuttings: purslane, mint, rose, chrysanthemum, basil. For basil, I prefer the hardier, aromatic African blue basil or the purple basil. In addition to the uses in Italian pesto and tomato sauce, it blends well in Thai laab and summer rolls.

Recipe

LEMON BASIL AND WILD LEMON BALM PESTO

July: suddenly it's hot and dry. The cucumbers are drooping, but the basil and the weeds are doing just fine. It's too hot to cook something heavy. I'm walking around the garden beds and I see some naturalized shiso, both green and red, some za'atar, feral mint, also lemon balm; in any given year I may have more of some and less of another. I like to mix some of the wild with some cultivated herbs for pesto with flavor and nuance. On a hot summer day I'm in the mood for a light and lemony herb pesto, mixing a cultivated lemon basil (or African spice basil) with wild lemon balm.

Pluck the leaves off the stems. (The stem is normally more bitter than the leaves.) I also tend to process it as little as possible, so that, unlike in a puree, the texture and freshness of the leaves brightens every bite.

INGREDIENTS

1 cup / 150 g raw pecan pieces

2 cloves garlic

6 cups / 180 g lemon basil leaves (I sometimes use African spice basil)

2 cups / 430 g grapeseed oil

2 cups / 60 g wild lemon balm leaves

2 cups / 180 g shredded Parmesan cheese

1 tablespoon salt (or to taste)

METHOD

1. In a food processor, pulse the nuts first. Scrape down the bowl.

2. Add the garlic and pulse.

3. Add the lemon basil and oil and pulse. Do not overblend.

4. Add the lemon balm and pulse just a few times. The lemon balm is soft and doesn't need much handling.

5. Stir in the Parmesan cheese and salt.

Mixes well with peas, shredded chicken, and pasta. As with any pesto, it freezes well.

TRAILING STEMS: ABOVEGROUND RUNNERS

Some stems do not grow upright but horizontally, running along the ground as runners, known as stolons. Some examples are ferns, creeping Jenny (*Lysimachia rummularia*), and goldmoss (*Sedum acre*). Sedums like to grow on rocks and cliff areas and also trailing on the edge of the driveway. I brought some *Sedum acre* inside. I made a shallow tray with *terroir de driveway*: two-thirds full of gravel and the top one-third potting soil, because the plant obviously likes a well-drained medium. I fashioned a grow light over it and in two weeks it had busted over the side of the tray and was forming little white rootlets on each node, searching for soil. I cut these and made another tray.

UNDERGROUND HORIZONTAL STEMS: RHIZOMES

Other noninvasive rhizomatous plants can be grown easily from the rhizome node. Some of my favorites are rau rum, passionflower, nettle, yarrow, and mint. If there is already an established rhizome with small rootlets, I do not even need to grow them out in water first.

The horizontal growth has nodes that grow rootlets that grow down into the ground and stem shoots that grow skyward. You want to make sure to plant the rhizome with the right section pointing up: when dividing a larger rhizome of a woody plant into four-inch sections, we make sure we keep track of which part of the stem was pointed up or down by making diagonal cuts on the rhizome for the part that was pointing down. You can remember D for diagonal and D for down, and pot the *diagonal* cut side *down* in potting soil.

Note: Tree cuttings and root cuttings are much more complex, and I find those are best left to the experts.

TRANSPLANTING WHOLE PLANTS

A beautiful flower blooming in the wild is tempting to dig up and bring home to plant. But you should not do this, for the following reasons:

1. When plants are in flower, they are at one of their weakest times to be dug out because a lot of the energy is being used to flower and go to seed. A mature flowering plant will experience great shock, and has not been conditioned to grow in some other place.

2. It is likely illegal to dig plants from public lands.

3. There is a high likelihood that the plant will eventually die in the new place, especially if it is a native plant and a so-called specialist that requires certain conditions of shade, soil, and moisture.

4. Conversely, if you have dug up an aggressive or invasive plant, it should not be spread to disrupt other habitats.

5. Digging out a plant destroys some of the feeder roots that bind the plant to the soil as well as the plant and wildlife associations with the surrounding plant habitat.

BUYING PLANTS TO TRANSPLANT AT HOME

I often fail at seed starting, and some plants don't grow well from cuttings, so I always supplement with a plant exchange or purchase starts from small specialty places.

When I go to a plant sale, I see people drawn to the tables with the biggest plants with showy, open flowers. I, on the other hand, beeline away from the crowds, toward plants with a small (four-inch) pot size, sturdy-looking green tops, and no flowers. I am thinking about the state of the plant underground: the roots. A plant in full bloom in a pot will experience greater shock when transplanted to a different environment. When you get the plant home, take it carefully out of the container and examine the root system: they should have fine tendrils and side roots that have soil clinging to them. If the plant has had too much time in the pot the plant may have become root bound. It is difficult for a nursery to time this right. A root-bound plant's roots have grown too big for the container and started encircling on each other, following the shape of the pot. These knots need to be broken apart so the roots can extend into the native soil. It's more important to untangle and trim the roots, even if some of the mass needs to be discarded.

Alternatively, if the plant's roots are not well formed, it will not survive a sudden transplant. Keep these plants in a cool area with some shelter and, similar to when transplanting your own seedlings from the outdoors into a pot, give them a chance to grow their roots out for at least two weeks before putting them in the ground. Moving plants around places stress on them.

A bare-root plant is dormant and not in a growth stage. It has been dug up from an outdoor bed, not from the wild, and stored by a nursery in a cool, controlled environment for shipping without soil or pots. Keep them moist, but not dripping, in a cool, dark place and plant as soon as you can. Bare-root plants will have a better adjustment if planted quickly from dormancy into a new place.

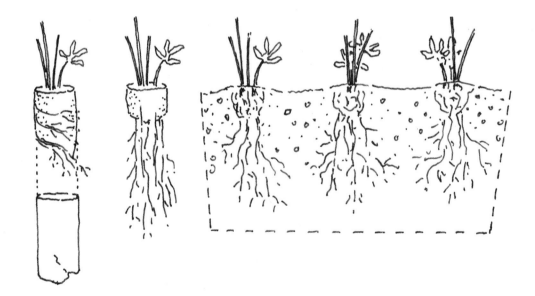

Trench Planting

If you have a good-size cluster of plants, particularly ones that are rhizomatous, such as yarrow, bee balm, and *Bidens*, instead of potting individual plants, try digging out a section in one clump 18–24 inches / 45.72–60.96 cm long by 8–10 inches / 20.32-25.4 cm wide. It doesn't have to be too deep, just enough that the tiny roots are also included.

Dig a shallow trench in a similar environment (e.g., sunny, part shade, moist, etc.) that will safely ensconce the clump. Backfill with extra garden soil. Water well. As the water dries, it will seal in the soil around the roots, so that no air pockets are left and the clump is well anchored.

I learned about this from giving plants to neighbors. I didn't have big enough plant containers, as I am not a plant nursery. But I didn't want to divide the cluster of plants, growing happily in concert, in native soil, exuberant and thriving. So, I just took out the whole chunk of soil, at least 1 foot / 30.48 cm square, from the garden bed, intact with several plants, their roots and little root feeders undisturbed, along with all the soil interactions and underground biome that helped them thrive so well in my garden. They have all done fabulously, and people who have received these plants marvel about how "strong" they are. It's not a secret, it's just that they have been transported along with their homes, belongings, and family as a whole, not separated. This worked so well with friends and neighbors that I started doing it myself. When I want to move the wild yarrow or American germander out of a bed and to another area, I just dig out a large clump of the entire plant section and put it in a hole I dug to fit the clump. Native soil meets native soil. In one week, the plants look as if they have always been there.

POCKET MEADOWS

Friends who stroll my wet meadows in season come away saying they "want one," but later on they tell me it didn't work, it was too hard. I had an open area next to the blooming wet meadow but for five years it looked like "nothing," meaning only ragged lawn and agricultural grasses, even after I tried the cool-season grass-mowing regime.

Some people hire a landscaper to install a meadow. This is not an inexpensive venture, and usually requires a complete herbicide application or two to get rid of the current plants, followed by a heavy seeding with, hopefully, appropriate native seed for the location, but usually not seed that is in situ of the local ecotype. People call me about these seedings seeming suspicious that something went wrong; where are the plants they expected? Are these the seeds or are these intruders?

If you want to kickstart a meadow by planting something you can try starting with a pocket meadow. Not too much, not a mulched construction, but plants that will start to introduce new elements and tip the balance away from those cool-season lawns and hay grasses. I'm talking about a small patch, but it will hopefully become a meadow like mine did.

You do not need to prepare the ground, but do choose a spot that is not covered with invasive species and is of the same conditions (wet/dry/sunny, etc.) as what you are planting came from. Plant on a cloudy day, but do not plant if the ground is **muddy**.

Roots should not be exposed to direct sunlight. Conversely, **muddy**, wet soil has no oxygen and will suffocate the new transplants.

I planted ten plugs of the native mountain mint *Pycnanthemum muticum*. Like most mints it spreads by rhizome, and I want it to spread because then I won't need to use mulch to keep out unwanted plants; this plant will do the work for me. The plant is not showy and doesn't shout at you from ten yards away, but when you pass by closely on any sunny day in the summer, stop and let your eyes adjust to skim the tops of the patch. You will start to see life where you thought there was nothing. Bumblebees, beneficial wasps, little butterflies, sweat bees, and sometimes honeybees, from miles around, having fun. Amazing. Then tear off a piece of a leaf. The mint is sharp and cuts through the air like a knife; when infused in tea it fades to a whisper of mint with herbaceous notes.

I bought the plugs from a local nursery and placed them right next to each other in a shallow trench, anticipating a clump, which formed nicely in a very short time. These clumps are relatively weed-free, because the ground in between is not disturbed or introduced to weed seeds.

The patch spread, and I started to notice other plants popping up. Over a couple of years the entire area was transformed. On the outer perimeter of the *Pycnanthemum* was a sister, narrow-leafed mountain mint (*Pycnanthemum tenufolium*). There was also Joe-Pye weed, a stand of big bluestem, and more recently a southern aster, sensitive fern, soft rush, and lavender bergamot (*Monarda fistulosa*). And no more lawn grass!

BRINGING PLANTS INDOORS

Some plants in my garden are not hardy in cold winters, though they grow all year in warmer climates. If you live in a warmer climate, you might want to bring plants indoors in scorching summers, like my friends living in Florida.

I like to bring non-cold-hardy perennials inside because it seems wasteful to keep replanting the same ones year after year. Bringing the plants in hedges my bets and also lets me eat fresh greens all winter long right out of my kitchen. Dig up a section of a plant to overwinter, keeping the current root system intact. Trim off the lower leaves.

Eligible transplants include longevity spinach (*Gynura*; see below), mint, za'atar (the herb), lemon verbena, parsley, and the weeds that accompany them in their trays and pots, such as chickweed, *Galinsoga*, upland cress.

Longevity spinach (*Gynura crepioiedes* or *G. procumbens*). I first ate this plant at a Szechuan noodle place on Hainan Island, China. It was listed on the menu as Wild Vegetable, and they served it room temperature with a little lime and vinegar; its mild but slightly piney flavor was a lovely counterpoint to the spicy noodle entrée. *Gynura* still grows wild in subtropical and tropical Asia, but the demand for this healthy vegetable is so great that it is now cultivated, though it still carries the cachet of wild origin.

Plants can be ordered online from specialty nurseries. The leaves can be harvested on a **cut-and-come-again** basis so that the plant does not become too floppy. After eating most of the leaves, snip off six-inch lengths and place the stems in a glass jar with unchlorinated water in a sunny windowsill. This plant likes moisture. When roots have grown out, plant in pots.

When I bring it indoors, I dig up the plant before frost and place in a large pot with a mixture of the soil it was growing in and potting soil, tamping down the soil and watering. I heavily trim off large leaves so that the plant will adapt easier to the new environment without having to support too much top growth for the roots to have to feed. The plant grows well all winter in a sunny window or underneath grow lights. It pairs well as a vegetable side dish with Szechuan noodles or curry and rice. It is a great indoor plant and indoor vegetable, and then I plant it outside again after frost.

Cut and come again is often used with certain types of lettuce to extend the season. The more mature leaves are harvested, allowing the younger shoots to send out new leaves.

LONGEVITY SPINACH

INGREDIENTS

8 leaves young *Gynura*

Lime juice, to taste

Rice vinegar or ponzu sauce, to taste

METHOD

1. Bring 2 cups / 473 g of water to a boil. Add the *Gynura* and blanch for a couple seconds until wilted.

2. Remove from the heat and drain. Tear or chop the leaves roughly.

3. Drizzle with lime juice and rice vinegar or a few drops of ponzu sauce. It pairs well as a vegetable side dish with Szechuan noodles, and can substitute for spinach.

LIME LEAF, GALANGAL, AND LEMONGRASS MEATBALLS

1 pound / 453.5 g coarse-ground pork

2 tablespoons light soy sauce

1 tablespoon fish sauce

½ cup / 30 g cilantro

5 makrut lime leaves, central rib removed and leaves finely sliced

1 tablespoon chopped lemongrass

1 teaspoon minced galangal (or substitute ginger)

½ teaspoon sugar

¼ teaspoon salt

Vegetable oil

1. Mix all the ingredients except the oil in a large bowl, until everything is well incorporated. Form the mixture into 1½-inch / 4 cm meatballs.

2. Heat the vegetable oil in a skillet and brown the meatballs in batches on all sides, turning.

3. Serve with rice and a sweet chile sauce or other fruity sauce.

Here are five things to do with fresh citrus leaves, which are commonly used in Southeast Asian cooking:

1. Twist a few whole leaves to release the oils and add to curries and soups in the same way bay leaves are used.

2. Twist and add to a cup of hot tea.

3. Remove the central rib of the leaf, which can be fibrous, and finely mince or roll and chiffonade, then add raw to fresh salads and lettuce leaf wraps.

4. Add citrus flavor when grilling meat, fish, or vegetable steaks: Once the steak is half cooked, in a grill pan, layer the top with citrus leaves. Flip the steak over leaf-side down and grill for an additional 2 minutes, until the leaves are softened and slightly charred. Remove from the pan and serve.

5. Use them in meatballs or burgers.

Grow Lights

In the dim winter days and long nights, plants, especially citrus, can use an extra light boost. Yet I don't want to spend the rest of the year with lots of unused lights and other paraphernalia oozing out of every corner of the house. This is simple to put together and just as simple to disassemble when I no longer need it (April through October in New Jersey; your season may be a little different). · **This will cover a growing area of about 2½ feet / 81.28 cm square, or enough for 5 pots.**

Plug-in hanging light kit, hanging light with plug-in cord, or industrial pendant light fixture with on/off switch (substitute: unused floor or desk lamps; just switch the bulbs)

Stick or rod, 4 feet / 1.22 m long and sturdy enough to hold the hanging light fixture

One bag-sealing clip (the ones you use to close open bags of potato chips)

Duct tape

Stable object to affix the light to (I use an air filter machine)

1 SANSI brand LED full-spectrum grow-light bulb: 36 W LED 400 watt / 120 volt (for citrus or large trees) or 10 W LED 150 watt / 120 volt for herbs and rhizomes and seed starting

Attach the cord of the hanging light kit to the stick with the clip. Attach the stick to the stable object with the duct tape so that the light is 4–5 feet / 1.22–1.52 m off the ground. The light should be positioned so that it is pointed at the plants and around 12–24 inches / 30.48–60.96 cm away. You can shift the position of the lamp by retaping the stick up or down as the plant grows.

Screw the bulb into the socket of the light kit, turn it on, and adjust the position. The light should be on 12–16 hours a day. I bring my handful of citrus trees off the porch in the winter as well.

PLANT RESCUE

 I have a thing for unwanted plants. The garden can be a place for refugees from the arbiters of the popular trends.

It started with violets. *Viola* is a romantic genus of plants that includes the cream violet, the yellow wood violet, and the swamp violet with petals rising gracefully on a long swan's neck of a stem. But I am equally captivated by the common violet scattered throughout many lawns and gardens, *Viola sororia*. You can find common violets in so many colors: from a deep blue-violet, to reddish-purple, and the confederate violet flecked with blue and gray. What's not to lose your heart to? But there is no accounting for taste, so when a friend said his daughter had asked him to rid her garden of the unwanted violets there, he remembered that my voice softens and gets all reverent when I say the word *violet*. He asked me if he could transplant them at my place. It took two or maybe three years in a row to rid her garden of the violets. We would keep them in pots, watered, and out of direct sunlight until they settled (about two weeks). We planted them and they "took" and flowered, but they didn't thrive. Over the next three years, they started to be crowded out by grass, ajuga, and other plants, so whereas they had been "thugs" in the neighbor's garden, at my place they had a different behavior. That is, until I saw a spread of violets in a semi-open sandy bed about fifteen feet away! It is now wall-to-wall violets where there were

none before—just not where we had planted them. I consider these plants "rescued," but what really happened is that they established roots in their new home as a second generation spread by ants—that second generation found its own spot to colonize and call home. Although common violet is known to spread underground by rhizome as well, it doesn't seem to have acted that way in my rescue situation.

NURSERIES

Nurseries often need to dispose of some stock, especially given the cost of having to overwinter a plant. I rescued two (labeled) potted cream violets (*Viola striata*) from a local native plant sale ten years ago. They have since spread profusely.

CONSTRUCTION SITES, VACANT LOTS, AND ROADSIDES

Ground is always being cleared for development, and I have rescued small juniper trees and taken sumac cuttings from sites under construction. I remember once, word spread that a beautiful patch of wild goldenseal was slated to be dug up for housing. I planted a few, but, while they are surviving, they are not thriving. It could be because of the difficulties of transplanting a specialist plant like goldenseal from the wild. I never try to move specialist plants, such as delicate spring ephemeral bloodroots, around to where it will complement the patio, for example, because by now I know they will surely die. I have bought some spring ephemerals as potted plants from reputable native plant nurseries, but over a decade they have not persisted, though my wild ones have.

So, even though I can never be quite sure these somewhat unplanned "rescues" will save a plant's life, I am always on the lookout. I'm never bored in traffic jams. Traffic jams force you to slow down, instead of whizzing by in a blur. As I inch along, I scope out what is growing alongside the highway shoulders and in the medians. The slower the crawl, the more detail I can see. Not only am I impressed with the resilience of these plants under some of the most challenging conditions, but some of my favorites (like sumac and juniper) persist there, perhaps because other garden plantings cannot. I secretly long to rescue highway plants, plants that will soon come under the knife of the mower, the tree chopper, or worse, the chemical sprayer, because they are blocking the view of cars. I have taken seed from these places so that they can be rescued to a place where they will not be killed. I wish that there could be a program with like-minded people working with the state highway people in charge to enable this. So much to do.

CHAPTER NINE

Preserving BOUNTY

WILD HARVEST PROTOCOLS 188

FREEZING 189

Ⓐ Prepare Leafy Greens for Freezing 190

Ⓡ Sour Cherry and Wild Berry Jam 191

SYRUPS 192

Ⓡ Spruce Tip Mocktail 192

Ⓡ Fig Leaf Gimlet 194

SHRUBS 197

Ⓡ Mulberry Shrub 197

FRUIT SPREADS 198

Ⓡ Feral Apple Spread 199

DRYING 200

WHEN THE SEASON is ON, I can tell by the tone in Derek's voice. Derek lives on the south side of the lands we forage, so he usually sees the plants' growth first. This time, when he calls, his Hello is long and melodious, "Hell...ooooo," and at the end there is a kind of chuckle. That is the chuckle of glee. Most people around here enjoy corn and tomato season, and when cucumbers and zucchinis bulge on the vine. But I am not sure that farmers feel the same kind of bliss that we do. Because we have not invested in planning, purchasing, seeding, and preparing for the fruits of labor, we think of our foods as more of a hoped-for blessing, unbidden by us, from the land.

From at least March to November, something is roaring for us. I can't imagine what it would be like to have only one main crop, because by the eighth week of picking many pounds of a plant—and weeds always seem to be in a glut—I frankly am a little weary of that plant. I don't want to see another nettle leaf, smell another wild maitake, or pick another pawpaw. And then, suddenly, the season is over. If I forgot to store some away, that's it until next year. It's not like I can just pop into the store to find it when I want. The bounty of the season goes too fast. In a last-minute rush, I always try to save a stash.

WILD HARVEST PROTOCOLS

Vegetable farmers have years of experience bringing bounty in from field to market. Foragers, on the other hand, often focus up front on identification and less so on what happens after they cut a plant. Ian, from a long line of Pennsylvania vegetable farmers, told me how plants retain the heat of the field even after they are brought indoors; he needs to spread them out and put them under refrigeration, aerated but covered. For tender greens and edible flowers, food safety sites give it one hour. But after the trouble of picking, we don't just want it to be safe, we want it to be crisp, juicy, vibrant. A tender leaf or shoot, picked on a bright day, can wilt in a minute. Avoid the hottest times of the day and never leave cut plants sitting exposed to the sun. It's a big deal. Even though these plants are survivors out in the wild, like wild animals, the transition to indoor soilless conditions may require different protocols than you would use with plants that have been cultivated to withstand machine harvest and warehouse storage.

Remember also the character of the plant: leafy greens need to be contained in something (like a roomy plastic bag or container) that will hold moisture in. Flowers also need to be put in something that holds moisture, maybe with a little spritzing. Berries, mushrooms, and fruits have their own quirks; mostly they need to be well aerated and have moisture kept away, not in. Paper bags, cardboard containers, and bins with airholes work well for this.

FREEZING

LEAFY GREENS

Except for peas, I never need to buy frozen vegetables to get greens. Wild leafy greens such as wild *Brassica rapa*, lambsquarters, and amaranth hold their texture and flavor extremely well after freezing. I use these healthy greens in omelets, Asian noodle dishes, with pasta, and as accompaniments for roasts. See page 190 for tips on freezing leafy greens.

FRUITS

- *Berries:* Wild blueberries freeze well in vacuum bags, and do not need to be laid flat. More fragile berries such as wineberries will hold their structure if spread first in a layer on a baking sheet and placed in the freezer. Once frozen, slide them into a vacuum-sealing bag.

- ***Fruits with pits such as beach plums and found cherries:*** I pit them first, then freeze on a large baking sheet. This preserves the texture of the fruit so it is less messy.

- *Pawpaws:* I carefully remove the skin and seeds and then puree and place in one-cup packs that I can use in baking and desserts.

Prepare Leafy Greens for Freezing

1. In a medium pot, bring water to a boil. Roughly chop the wild vegetables, removing any large, stiff stems.

2. Plop the wild vegetables in the water for only a few seconds or until the color turns bright green. Drain in a strainer with ice to prevent overcooking.

3. Freeze and label in vacuum-sealed bags to prevent freezer burn.

SOUR CHERRY AND WILD BERRY JAM

I always try to have some sour cherries from the farmers' market on hand, but the timing may not align with the season for blueberries or other wild berries (such as serviceberries or wineberries), so I freeze the cherries first and then use them in this jam. This is a small-batch jam that doesn't require much time boiling. Also, depending on how dense the berries are, I may add pectin for a firmer jam, or not.

INGREDIENTS

2 cups / 380 g pitted sour cherries

2 cups / 380 g blueberries or serviceberries

2 cups / 380 g raspberries, blackberries, or wineberries

½ cup / 237 g water

2 tablespoons lemon juice

2 cups / 400 g sugar

METHOD

1. Combine all the fruits in a large nonreactive pot and add water.

2. Bring to a boil.

3. Add the lemon juice.

4. Add the sugar ½ cup / 100 g at a time, letting the sugar dissolve between each addition and return to a boil.

5. Within 10 minutes the jam will thicken. Remove from the heat and transfer to hot sterilized jam jars.

6. Invert the jars to set the seal. Alternatively, place the filled and closed jars in a boiling water bath and leave submerged for 8 minutes.

SYRUPS

Syrups are a liquid, no-pectin version of jellies and jams. While I don't prefer foods that are too sweet and "syrupy," sugar is an old-fashioned way to preserve food. In addition, macerating with sugar is a fine way of extracting flavor.

Recipe

SPRUCE TIP MOCKTAIL

Spruce tips freeze well, so you can keep the piney refreshing flavor around for a summer drink. Because the spruce has an already potent flavor, it does not need to be macerated first with the sugar. This is my favorite take on a lime soda.

Spruce Tip Syrup

YIELD: Approximately 2 cups / 475 ml

INGREDIENTS

2 cups / 473 g water

2 cups / 400 g sugar

1 cup / 50 g frozen spruce tips

METHOD

1. Heat the water and sugar and stir until the sugar is dissolved (do not boil as that will evaporate the water and throw off the proportions, making the sugar more concentrated).

2. Let cool.

3. Blend the syrup and spruce tips on high for ten seconds, or until it turns a frothy lime-green color.

4. Strain with a fine sieve into mason jars. Seal and refrigerate.

TO MAKE A MOCKTAIL FOR ONE

INGREDIENTS

1 oz. / 30 ml lime juice (from 2 fresh limes; do not substitute lemons)

1 oz. / 30 ml Spruce Tip Syrup

Optional: 1 oz. / 30 ml gin

Tonic water, for topping

METHOD

1. Fill a shaker with ice.

2. Add the lime juice, spruce tip syrup, and gin (if using), and shake.

3. Pour into a highball glass with a lot of ice cubes.

4. Fill the rest of the glass with high-quality tonic water.

5. Enjoy outdoors on a hot day.

FIG LEAF GIMLET

My eyes light up whenever I see a fig tree. But I am not looking at the fruits. Feral trees in California or planted trees in the East never or hardly ever produce fruit. But these "failed" fig trees have giant lobed leaves. Watch out to avoid the milky sap when cut (some people may be allergic, but also because it's just generally kind of yucky and sticks on things). The leaves have a coconut-vanilla-green smell that is so enticing you want to bottle it up. I wait until after the height of the fruit season and before the leaves fall off for the winter (the tree is not evergreen), then I gather the leaves and make them into syrup or freeze them. The leaves keep well, but the syrup tastes better with recently ground leaves, so I make a batch of syrup within a week of grinding them.

A gimlet is a cocktail that usually uses lime juice with simple syrup. Here, instead of simple syrup we use fig leaf syrup, which adds a freshness and smoothness to the cocktail. How do you describe the taste of fig leaf? A little coconutty, vanilla-y, and herbal.

Fig Leaf Syrup

YIELD: Approximately 5 cups / 1 L syrup

INGREDIENTS

15–20 fresh or frozen fig leaves (125 g)

5 cups / 1,000 g sugar

(4¼ cups) / 1,010 g water

METHOD

1. Roughly tear the fig leaves up into 4-inch / 10.16 cm pieces or smaller for easier grinding.

2. Add the sugar.

3. Grind the leaves together with the sugar FIRST in batches in a food processor on high. (Pastry chef Rebecca Ellis taught me this, and bartenders have been asking us for this secret for years. So here it is.) The mixture should look like a green sugary mix. Do not boil the sugar and water and then throw a fig leaf in.

4. In a large pot, combine the mixture with the water and heat until the sugar is dissolved, stirring so that it does not stick to the bottom.

5. Turn off the heat and let infuse for a minimum of 4 hours, or overnight.

6. Strain, bring the strained green liquid just to a boil, transfer to mason jars, and seal.

TO MAKE A COCKTAIL FOR ONE:

INGREDIENTS

2 oz. / 59 ml gin
¾ oz. / 22 ml Fig Leaf Syrup
¾ oz. / 22 ml freshly squeezed lime juice

METHOD

1. Fill a cocktail shaker with ice.

2. Add the gin, syrup, and lime juice.

3. Shake vigorously until the mixture is very cold.

4. Strain over ice and serve right away.

SHRUBS

A shrub is a tart mixture made with vinegar that can be used to preserve berries and fruits. I keep a few jars in the refrigerator and use them to perk up water, soda, and cocktails all year long. This one is adapted from my friend Connie Green's recipe for shrub:

Recipe

MULBERRY SHRUB

YIELD: Approximately 4 cups / 920 g

INGREDIENTS

2 cups / 332 g wild mulberries

1 cup / 200 g sugar

1 cup / 230 g red wine vinegar (for white mulberries, substitute champagne vinegar)

METHOD

1. In a medium pot, combine the ingredients and bring just to a boil.

2. Turn down the heat and simmer on low for about 5 minutes until the mulberry consistency is soft and mushy.

3. Use the back of a wooden spoon to press on the berries.

4. Strain out the berries.

5. Refrigerate the shrub.

TINCTURES

Tinctures are a way of preserving in alcohol that has been practiced for centuries to make bitters, elixirs, and other concoctions.

Try making your own tinctures by submerging spices, herbs, fruit, or vegetables in a 151-proof neutral grain spirit for at least two weeks, and up to a year. Once you like the flavor, strain and store in an airtight container.

FERMENTS

Fermentation is an ancient method of preservation that relies on bacteria, yeasts, or other micro-organisms to break down sugar.

Try making your own fermented syrup by combining 2 cups / 473 ml of fruit or flowers with ¾ cup / 50 g sugar and 1 cup / 237 ml water in a mason jar, covering loosely with a breathable cloth, and storing in a cool dark place. Check and resubmerge the mass every few days until it starts to bubble and turns delightfully tart, then strain and refrigerate in an airtight container.

FRUIT SPREADS

Feral trees are often trees that were not planted but have been naturalized; that is, gone wild from planted trees. One of my favorites are feral apple trees. Apples are not indigenous to North America, so any tree you come across is not truly "wild" but rather descended from a cultivated apple. I don't actively look for apple trees, but there are plenty around wherever winters are cold enough: besides fallow orchards and occasional plantings, I sometimes find truly feral trees on the edges of woods and overgrown fields. If it is a good apple year, you can't be outdoors and not notice them, particularly north of the Mid-Atlantic area. The comments I always read about these feral apples, though, or even apples at untended old orchards, are that the fruit is small, sometimes wormy, and sour. But last year was such a bumper year they were falling on my head and littering the ground in the Northeast, and I could no longer ignore their potential.

The first thing I noticed was that it was difficult to tell ripeness from the color because they weren't completely red, like in the grocery store, or completely green. After trial and error, I found that they were ripe when they easily slipped off the tree branch and I didn't have to tug, or when they were newly fallen (before critters or dampness had their way with them).

I gathered a bushelful to try. I sliced into one. Completely clean and firm. Firmer than most of the apples that I bought at the supermarket. I would characterize them as smaller but denser, with less water content, and that contributed to their extra crispness. Delicious as a very thin slice, but yes, a quite tart "kick" at the end.

Now, these feral apples will vary immensely, as apples do, so you will have to do your own trial and error, but I found an easy way to cook them up for your pantry; it surpasses any applesauce you can buy, or I will eat my forager's hat.

FERAL APPLE SPREAD

I call this a spread because it is thicker than a sauce but thinner than a butter or paste. That's really up to you, though. I didn't want to cook it down further to make a butter, which also would be browner and more sugary. This was the perfect in-between for me. I did not add spices because I wanted to use this as a base for many dishes: I have now used it as a Thanksgiving side, just as it is, but you can also add it to butternut squash/apple/curry soup, use it in cranberry-apple upside-down cake, or sub it in anytime you would ordinarily use applesauce. This is a rich red color and has zing. I wonder who invented the supermarket applesauce with its bland flavor and wheatlike color...surely no one who has made feral apple spread!

Also, since we were not at our house, I scrounged around in the kitchen and found a couple of old tools for the job: a hand blender and a large slow cooker. I am sure that you can use whatever you have on hand to achieve similar results, but this worked incredibly well for me.

YIELD: 5 pints / 2.37L

TOOLS

Slow cooker

Immersion blender

INGREDIENTS

5 lb. / 2.26 kg apples, cored, destemmed but NOT skinned, and cut in large chunks

1 cup / 200 g sugar

1 tablespoon lemon juice

METHOD

1. Place the apples, sugar, and lemon juice in the slow cooker.

2. Set the cooker for 5 hours on low. Open the lid and check that it is the thickness you desire.

3. Blend with the hand blender for about 25 seconds.

DRYING

Drying is a most ancient method of preserving food. In almost any village culture, vegetables, meat, and fish are salted and hung up to dry on racks, roofs, and rafters and bake in the sun.

HERBS AND LEAFY GREENS

Choose a room for drying, preferably on the second floor, airy, with indirect light. Run a dehumidifier in this room. Keep the humidity monitor at around 40 percent. If you control the humidity, you can air-dry herbs on screens in this room. Once dry and crisp, I store the whole herbs in large cardboard boxes, only half full. If the boxes are not airy enough, the bottom layer may become compressed and potentially funky.

WOOD, NEEDLES, MUSHROOMS, AND FRUIT

I need a hunter-size dehydrator with a temperature control to provide adequate air circulation to dry my voluminous plant matter. It usually requires a minimum setting of about 130°F / 54°C for mushrooms or wood, and higher for fruit. Although we have exact specifications for our needs, it will vary depending on how moist the item is when you put it in, how dense it is, and the external environment. If necessary, we use a moisture meter to be sure an item is ready for longer-term storage.

Unlike many cultivated nuts, wild nuts, cones, and berries are not treated or sprayed and may commonly host a number of hungry critters, especially weevils. These are microscopic, but when exposed to a nice warm environment they can grow fat and big. Ripe juniper berries (*Juniperus virginiana*) contain a lot of oils that at a certain stage attract weevils. We first freeze the ripe berries for about three days and then dry them in a commercial dehydrator at 140° / 60°C for about two hours or until dried; if we dehydrate first, the weevils grow explosively overnight and the next morning we find them lounging all over the dehydrator. Green juniper berries will keep for two weeks if left on the branch in a cool, dark, airy box.

CHAPTER TEN

Creating MEMORIES

THE CULTURE OF TEA 205

Ⓡ   Honeysuckle Tea 206

CEREMONIALS 211

Ⓐ   Using Wild Plants in Arrangements 212

Ⓟ   Chicken Wire Flower Frog 216

Ⓟ   Wildflower Leis 218

Ⓐ   Smudge Sticks 222

Ⓟ   Juniper Firestarters 223

THE CULTURE
OF TEA

As I write this, my father is ninety-three with advanced dementia, confined to a wheelchair and unable to speak in full sentences. He knows us; he knows he is home and not in an institution. In these later years of a full life, he enjoys simple things, the important things: a single flower petal, the rain on the roof, the trees rustling. His eyes track the pattern of a bird in flight. Every day my father relishes eating outdoors, al fresco, a fresh egg with wild greens, or rice porridge with fermented mustard greens and wild chives. He lounges outside, enjoying what we call *komorebi* (the dance of dappled sun through the trees and leaves). The outdoors is a place of healing and is especially beneficial for persons with depression, dementia: he experiences the garden holistically, with the sounds of birds and bumblebees, the aromas and the touch of the breezes. He is remembering things, and I am also creating memories with him, surrounded by wild things, healing myself.

Gatherings, ceremonies, and celebrations using wildflowers and other seasonal materials etch memories and distill them into a time and place: the mood, the colors, the scents become something unforgettable.

I come from a tea-drinking culture and never drink coffee, just wake up—*ping*—at dawn, with the first rays of light.

The culture of tea predates coffee by thousands of years, and leads back to China; the story goes that a leaf from a wild tree, *Camellia sinensis*, floated into the emperor's cup of hot water. The emperor was an herbalist and inspired by the aroma and flavor of the infusion. And so, from these beginnings, tea has spilled over to the rest of the world and become thoroughly embedded in the customs of people, their social life, and health. Tea means a simple roasted millet hot drink in the highland trails of Nepal, as well as a Japanese warm whisked matcha ceremony with a hundred formal variations. In both cases, tea satisfies both the mind and the body and is restorative to both.

So tea started with a wild botanical, and in that spirit, how fitting it is to wander out to the wildish garden to pick some leaves for a tisane. Savor a cup for yourself or share a tea for two. Remember the moment.

I start with a very mild infusion (light and not dark), no more than one cup a day. You are sipping this tea, not guzzling it. Everything in moderation. In tea drinking, the line between refreshment and tonic is often a matter of potency. The darker and longer the steep, the more potent. Chinese medicinal teas are very dark and potent, and meant to be so, with very specific ratios for tinctures and mixtures. The tea called Iron Buddha is so strong it is usually consumed in a miniature teacup something like a shot glass, at the end of a long Chinese multicourse meal.

THE ESSENTIALS FOR MAKING GOOD TEA

- **Water:** Naturally, water is the main ingredient in tea. Good water. Preferably spring water, without chlorine or additives. Don't make too large a batch.

- **Heat:** Leaves with more fragile flavor should not be boiled, and water that is rushing—poured over the leaves with lots of oxygen—is good.

- **Steeping time:** To taste.

- **Teapot:** Clay is the best conductor for holding heat, although you can also buy inexpensive cups with lids that hold the heat well.

- **Whole-leaf tea:** Crush lightly to release the oils before steeping.

- ***Metal tea strainer:*** There are many types on the market, but they should last forever and should be dishwasher safe.

- ***Note:*** Tea-drinking Asian households with electricity rely on a hot water dispenser; these are now available with stainless steel insides. Unlike a teakettle, it holds the water at a certain hot temperature. I just push the button when I want tea and strain into the cup.

Recipe

HONEYSUCKLE TEA

The flowers of the Asian honeysuckle vine (*Lonicera japonica*; *jinyinhua* in Chinese) are used in an ancestral recipe for a medicinal, "cooling" tea with a sweet aroma. Notice that on a stem the flowers do not all open at the same time. The flowers at the ends of the vine will be still budding while the flowers further up are open. Dry both the buds as well as the opened flowers, gently.

Combine 1 tablespoon dried honeysuckle flower with 1 tablespoon green tea leaves in 3 cups / 710 g hot water. Add honey to taste, if desired.

Note: Traditional Chinese medicine purists use only the green and white closed buds, reputed to have antiviral properties, in their tea.

Ode to the Chrysanthemum

"Tasting chrysanthemum tea of old—this flower of longevity! A man of eighty years picks and sips, assiduous; Teaching his frosty beard to turn raven black."—ZHENG BAN-QIAO

When I saw the mums for sale in the store, I didn't give them a second glance. I guess they looked so prefabricated that I didn't connect them with the flowers of the poetic *kiku* (the crest of the emperor of Japan), so I fell off my chair when I checked and found that indeed, the Juhua or kikuka species, *Chrysanthemum morifolium*, is the same species that has now been bred, hybridized into different colors and shapes, and sold commonly in the fall as "mums." They are descended from the chrysanthemums eaten and revered as an artistic inspiration; as a flower for tea, the shoots and roots for medicinal purposes.

There are many other species of *Chrysanthemum*, so I make sure to purchase *morifolium* or *nankingese*, as I am not confident about the edible tea properties of the others. I also don't plan to consume the blooms of the ones for sale as ornamentals, as they weren't grown or treated with edibility in mind. Instead, I grow them from plugs.

GROWING CHRYSANTHEMUMS IN THE GARDEN

Aside from purchasing some starter plants (not yet in bloom) from a reputable nursery, chrysanthemums can be divided off a couple plants with roots in warm weather and placed in water in a bottle in a sunny window. Once you see roots, you can pot them up; let them root out in the pot for about a month, and then plant them in your garden any time in spring after the last frost but before September. Once you have a rooted, healthy plant, you can consume some of the shoots, leaving other shoots to grow taller and bloom. Once blooming, snip off the flowers and remove the outside green parts. The flower petals can be scattered over salads and fish. Or, as in China, just dry the entire top flower plus the greens for tea.

Since I hate the extra effort of planting and replanting annuals (laziness, frugality), I don't plan to throw away the mums after they stop flowering. I also don't plan to "cut them back" and bring them indoors for the winter. The New York Botanical Garden advises: "Don't cut your mums back until spring...[p]inch mums in late May or June when the shoots are 6 inches tall to encourage branching and a bushier habit. Pinch again when the shoots are 3–6 inches tall...or just wait and cut the plants in half by late June above a leaf node." (To me, "pinching" sounds like forager harvesting.)

SOME FAVORITE PLANTS FOR DRIED WHOLE-LEAF TEA

- *Sweet fern (Comptonia peregrina):* I think this is one of my favorite teas, especially in the morning, but I struggle to describe the aroma: complex, spicy notes, like a Syrah, sweet-tangy...

- *Passionflower (Passiflora incarnata):* I dry the entire plant before frost. The flavor is very mild, so I add a mint or lemon balm leaf to the tea for some kick. Medicinally reputed to have a calming, antianxiety effect.

- *Sumac (Rhus typhina):* Dip brick-red fruit headfirst in warm to hot water. Let steep until the water turns deep pink. Strain. Refrigerate. To serve, add a splash of fresh lemon juice and agave.

- *Pineapple weed (Matricaria discoidea):* When dry it is similar to chamomile tea.

- *Stinging nettle (Urtica dioica):* The flavor is green, herbal, fresh. Medicinally, it is reputed to boost the immune system, and it has been used to treat arthritis, gout, and urinary problems.

CEREMONIALS

WILD ARRANGEMENTS

Plant arrangements are tied to all important cultural passages. Flowers and plants are arranged in places of remembrance and homage in many traditional homes. Ivy Wong, my mother-in-law, kept an alcove in the side bedroom where photos of the grandmothers and grandfathers were displayed with a thoughtful flower arrangement, dried or seasonal. We would always pay our respects to this little altar of ancestors when we came to visit and before going to visit the ancestral graves. On the Japanese side of my family, their traditional house has a spartan room where the place of honor is in a small alcove, *tokonoma*, displaying ikebana arrangements of seasonal plants and flowers. A thread of incense, thin and woody, lingers; the room is filled with the scent of soft rush mats. We sit in silent reflection, with legs and toes folded under.

White flowers are often the color of purity in weddings in the West; white is the color for funerals in Buddhist ceremonies.

Using Wild Plants in Arrangements

The display of flowers at heart is a deeply religious offering to the heavens, a spiritual reciprocation of nature's beauty. When preparing the plants for an offering, the focus is on significance, not decoration. In ancient China, the symbolism involved the rule of three: the entire universe was contained in the triangle. So, in arrangements, flowers should not be all the same height; one must be taller and the other two shorter; or one tall, one medium, one short. And the composition was meant to capture the mood of the season and idealize nature in a single flower or a set of flowers. *Ikebana* means "living flower"; its principles follow wabi-sabi and honor themes found throughout nature: asymmetry (points of three) and the ephemerality of life, reflected in the season.

Materials

Knife and scissors

5-gallon / 18.92 L bucket

Water, preferably unchlorinated

Vessel that can hold water: bowl, vase, or clear glass

Kenzan (pin-style flower frog) or **chicken wire formed to fit the vessel you select**

Clear work surface

1. **Gather the plants.** When gathering plants, reflect on the local micro season. What is the mood of the moment? Are small branches in bud? Are any leaves turning color? Are some plants seeding or just starting to form flowers? Walk around outdoors and collect items that reflect the moment, including bolted vegetables such as mustards or herbs such as coriander or flowering basil. Collect more than you think you will need for plenty of choices. My cousin Akiko and I went a little crazy gathering invasive plants. Wisteria vine, bittersweet, multiflora rose hips, privet, autumn olive, burning bush. She was excited to see these plants here in New Jersey, and the state of New Jersey was so pleased to give us a special use permit to harvest them. They even provided "priority" (read: challenging) sites to begin work on.

2. **Enjoy the process of selecting plants.** I like to find a plant in the process of change. The flower buds are starting to shoot up, some

fruits starting, leaves turning. Notice multiple shades of green: yellow green feels sunny; a dark green throws shade. Tip: for flowers, it is best to try to pick in the morning and when they are not fully open, leaving time for them to open later.

3. Fill the bucket halfway, with at least 4 inches / 10.16 cm of water. Remove any lower foliage and immediately immerse stems in water.

4. **The "landing" stage.** Wild plants need some adjustment time to adapt to an indoor environment, more so than cultivated plants that have been bred and treated to acclimate to a warehouse. With a very sharp knife, snip each stem again diagonally while it is in the water. This increases the surface area so they can absorb water more readily.

5. **Tip:** if the plant continues to wilt, there may be air captured in the stem and blocking the water absorption. Try burning the end of the stem and recutting the end under water. For branches: make a small slit in the bottom of the branch. For thin branches, peel the skin to expose the surface so the plants can drink in more water.

6. Leave the plants in the bucket for several hours to hydrate, or optimally, overnight in a cool location, away from direct sunlight.

7. In the meantime, consider the form the arrangement might take. What vessels would complement the gatherings? Low and shallow bowls, or taller and vase-like? Consider where you plan to set the arrangement and the size of the vessel against the setting. Avoid placing in direct sunlight.

There are myriad easy methods to use in working with wild plants. Here I describe three examples that I personally use. I have categorized them based on the method of stabilizing the plants inside the water-holding vessel: 1) simple—no holder, 2) structured, using a *kenzan* (flower frog), and 3) loose, using chicken wire.

In all methods, the key is to clear a work area of distractions and free your thoughts and your mood so that the process of arranging itself is one of focus and repose. Remember to select stems in groups of threes and to make it interesting by playing on an asymmetrical structure. The spaces between the elements—known as *ma*—are just as important, like the pauses between notes in music.

Simple: This technique uses bud vases or glass containers; no holder required. Three violets perched on long stems, lesser celandine early-spring flowers of yellow sunshine, or a single umbellifer-type head such as wild fennel, Queen Anne's lace, or dill can be quite expressive in this simple form.

Structured: This technique uses a flower frog called a *kenzan*, a heavy metal pincushion that sits in the bottom of a dish or plate; the "pins" are so close together that they hold plant stems in place and are better suited to upright plants with some vertical interest. The kenzan originated in Japan.

How to use a kenzan: Press the horizontally cut stem of the flower into the flower frog (it doesn't matter if the stem is in between pins or exactly on a pin). If you want the stem to slant in one direction, first press the stem vertically and then gently slant the stem by pushing on the bottom so as not to break the stem. Wider branches or twigs can be cut with a slit at the bottom to give more stability in the kenzan.

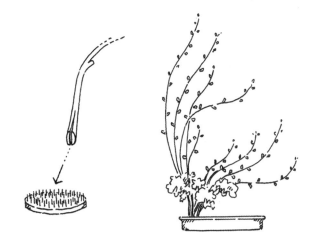

Select a shallow bowl or dish as your vessel.

Thinking in threes, select a taller stem or branched form, and press the bottom into the kenzan. Add a medium-height plant and then lower flowers around the base. The flowers should face the viewer and not point up.

Fill the vessel to about one inch with cool, clean water.

TIP: If the kenzan moves around in the vessel or there is a heavy mass of plants covering the frog that might tip it over, secure it to the bottom of the vessel with florist's putty.

Loose: This technique, known as *nageire* ("thrown in"), still starts with the rule of threes but could also expand to five or another odd number, meaning it should still not look too perfect or symmetrical. This style does not use the kenzan but instead a loose grid, such as a chicken wire base, into which the stems are inserted and stabilized. This style can also be considered "full," because the wire can accommodate more stems. The fullness associated with a Western-style arrangement would also use this technique.

Chicken Wire Flower Frog

These work well in cases where you want a fuller arrangement. The final holder does not have to be perfect because no one is going to see the chicken wire. The wire is just a frame for holding the plants in the arrangement. · **This project will yield one medium-size (5 inches / 12.7 cm diameter and 4 inches / 10.16 cm high) round flower frog.**

MATERIALS

Chicken wire (with 1-inch / 2.54 cm cells), cut into a rectangle 14 by 7 inches / 35.56 by 17.78 cm

Vessel (an actual vase or something that serves as one)

Wire cutters

Floral tape

METHOD

1. Curl the longer sides of the wire rectangle inward so that they form a barrel or jelly roll shape. Twist the ends of the chicken wire to each other so that the roll is securely fastened.

2. Next, press down the top end of the roll so the points face in.

3. Press the top row of wire cells down, using an overlapping motion, going all around in a circle of rough pleats, somewhat similar to gift wrapping a cylinder-shaped present. Tuck in any stray wire ends. Do the same on the bottom row of wire cells.

4. Pat the wire into a shape that will suit the chosen vessel.

5. Place the chicken wire frog in the bottom of your vessel. Secure by making an X across the top with waterproof floral tape.

6. Pour cool water into the vase until halfway to the top.

7. Place each plant stem, one by one, through the chicken wire cells. The stems should be inserted around the grid, like a porcupine so it can be viewed from a 3-D perspective. Weaker stems can gain extra support by inserting through a double set of cells.

8. To care for the arrangement: Do not place in direct sunlight; replace water regularly.

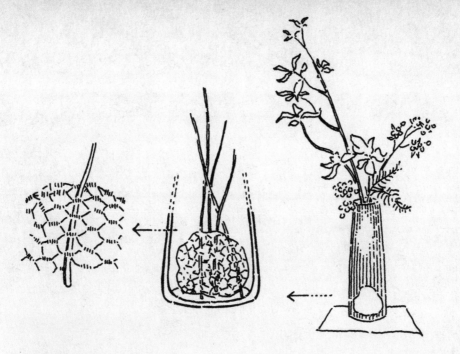

Use your own creativity to express the natural liveliness and exuberance of the plants.

1. **Colors.** Instead of trying to match the decor, select colors that reflect the mood of the season.

2. **Show variety by having plants in different life stages.** Instead of a "still-life" type of arrangement with flowers all in bloom, have a selection of a plant in bud, unfurling or young, immature, as well as plants in full bloom and in seed.

3. **Asymmetry and movement.** In ikebana, a given species is often represented in odd numbers, not even. This will naturally lead to a less symmetrical arrangement.

4. **The bottom of the arrangement.** Consider partly covering the vessel edge, so it doesn't form a "hard line" but instead lets the arrangement spill partly over the rim or hang down.

5. **The top of the arrangement.** The spaces at the very top corners of the arrangement are open. This is a good place to highlight and show off something especially alluring, such as the tips of a branch where the leaves are just emerging, or the top of a fiddlehead. If placed in the center of the arrangement, these beautiful elements could get lost.

6. **The center.** The center of the arrangement can also be lost. Highlighting a strong dominant flower and then having the background behind it darker will draw attention to this grounding point.

7. **Liveliness.** The top and outside edges of the arrangement can be quite effective in demonstrating liveliness and the mood. Having some extending elements adds movement and spirit to the arrangement.

8. **Set your arrangement in an area where the viewpoint is from the area where you want it to be seen.** If to be viewed only from the front, then place in an alcove.

Wildflower Leis

Flowers are an important part of culture in the tropics, where flowers grow wild in such profusion. Mom's cousins, aunties, and great uncles always greeted her with a fresh flower garland, a lei, when she took the long journey home to Honolulu. Aloha! The lei is a token of welcome and affection: used for celebrations, holidays, and anniversaries, but also just for simple occasions; and leis are cast into the sea on departing and in remembrance. My mother always tried to make a lei for our family on May 1, Lei Day. They did not have fresh orchids or tropical flowers in New Jersey, so, though they were not as perfumed, my mother made leis of plants and flowers she found around us. She also kept leis of dried shells and seedpods, strung together like beads. Traditionally, in Hawaii, leis were made with all kinds of natural and uncultivated plant materials, including milkweed flowers, chrysanthemum flowers, dodder, and vines.

A lei is usually 40 inches / 1 m in length in order for the finished piece to reach to the waist, but this is not a rule. You can adjust the measurements by first using a string to measure the desired length of your lei.

For this project, I used wild ajuga from the lawn, which was flowering in spring. It was a good choice because it had a stiff stem, which meant it would hold up well when strung; also, being in the mint family, it has a hollow square stem, perfect for easy threading. These leis use both the flowers and the stems to show two faces of the same plant and both lasted about three days. · **This project will yield one lei, 40 inches / 1.27 m in circumference.**

Lei needle, 12 inches / 30.48 cm (available online)

Lei thread (40 inches / 1 m)

8 cups / 200 g ajuga, cut into pieces about 4 inches / 10 cm long (pick extra to ensure you have enough)

METHOD

1. Thread the needle and tie a knot at the end of the thread.

2. Thread the needle through the stems of the plant, playing around with different patterns as well as how long each piece will be.

3. Tie the ends and drape as a garland or necklace.

ON AROMATICS AND CEREMONIES

The sense of smell is closely linked in the brain with memory. A certain aroma sparks the recall of an experience in a rush. When creating memories, the aroma is what will linger. There are at least ten dimensions of smells: fragrant, woody, minty, sweet, chemical, popcorn, lemon, fruity, pungent, decayed. The fragrance of a flower, the aroma of the essential oil of a plant, should be considered when selecting botanicals for ceremonial uses as well as for enhancing mood, as has been done since ancient times.

About twelve thousand years ago, the Natufians, of the Middle Ground, buried their kin on a bed of flowers—Judean sage, mint, and aromatic figwort—as a place of rest for their final journey. In modern times, two decades ago in New Jersey, when the girls were young, we kept assorted rabbits and chickens. One night something got into the rabbit hutch, and one died in the morning; the other, wounded, needed to be put down. It was somewhat of an awful moment amid a fair amount of suffering. In order to heal the spirit of the dead rabbit and our torn selves, we held a ceremony in the dry meadow, on top of the hillock. We dug a hole in the sand and laid down fresh grass in the bottom. We placed the rabbit tenderly in a bed of wild herbs and flowers, with a makeshift cross of twigs, and planted a Buddhist incense stick on top of the burial grounds. We said a few words of respect for the rabbit and to ease our troubles. Out in the middle of the summer meadow, the bees buzzed around us.

Monasteries and temples often have at their center a lovingly tended garden; the garden is a place of healing, respite, and meditation. Monastery gardens are also productive gardens, for spiritual ritual and also for eating the fruits of a spiritual life. It is important, spiritually, to eat from the labor of one's own hands: "you will eat the fruit of your labor, blessings and prosperity will be yours" (Psalm 128).

A wild garden, following the rhythms of change, is exuberant, it is solemn; it has spirit and is spiritual. The wild garden bestows gifts of meaning, not just ornament. Wild plants tell an ancestral story steeped in significance and ritual: birth, marriage, passing, holy days, riding off to battle, the beginning of peace. Or stories of occasion: a meal with family and friends, or even finishing a book. A reflection of a state of mind, a pause from the world.

The plants are a token of a moment, a specific time and place. Although they may be pleasing to the eye, they also may represent different times in a life, in your life, which adds to their meaning as you gather them from places around you.

Floriography is the secret or indirect communication of meanings through flowers. Certain flowers have certain significance and meanings, such as red roses for love, or yellow roses for friendship.

Smudge Sticks

Unlike the sweeter floral fragrances, woody and earthy aromas are reminiscent of the forest, wood, and fire, evoking feelings of warmth, grounding, and richness. Often these aromas are part of ancient ceremonies and also personal spiritual healing.

Smudging, or the burning of dried aromatic herbs, has been a practice to clear away the old/negative and bring in the new/positive. It is often used when entering a new house, as a welcome. Native Americans use white sage and other sage extensively. East Asian cultures smudge with mugwort; Europeans would hang mugwort in the eaves.

Cut plants. Hang to dry. Bundle with string. Light the end, then gently blow out the flame and let a thin column of smoke rise.

Use your own creativity and olfactory observation to find local materials for smudging. Here are some suggestions to get you started.

West: California bay and eucalyptus, western juniper, sages (but do not harvest wild white sage)

Northwest: mixed balsam and grand fir

Pine Barrens: camphorweed and white cedar, pitch pine resin, eastern red cedar

Herbs: *Artemisia annua* and sweet clover, mugwort

Juniper Firestarters

Juniper, aka eastern red cedar (*Juniperus virginiana*), burns hot and slow; it was a top fire plant used by Native Americans and is a component of natural firestarters today. The juniper tree is a weedy tree, and it is shade intolerant, so the lower branches often become shaded out from light and start to die back. These branches are low and easy to gather, and make great firewood, instead of purchasing firewood products.

Lop off the lower branches at about 1 inch / 2.54 cm diameter and dry them at around 140°F / 60°C. Drying time will vary depending on how wet the wood is and the size of the branches, but they will be dry enough when the needles fall off easily. · **This project will yield one firestarter.**

MATERIALS

1 juniper branch, 3 feet / 1 m long and approximately 1 inch / 2.54 cm diameter, cut into 4 lengths of about 9 inches / 23 cm

Brown wrapping paper, 24 by 18 inches / 46 by 61 cm

Twine

METHOD

1. Dry the juniper lengths in a dehydrator at 130°F / 54°C overnight or until the needles fall off.

2. Place the bundle of juniper on the paper and roll it, overlapping the ends.

3. Twist one end and secure with twine.

4. Twist the other end and secure with twine. Now your firestarter is ready to throw on the hearth.

CHAPTER ELEVEN

The FUTURE IS UNKNOWN

THE HUMAN FOOTPRINT now dominates the earth, in this age of the Anthropocene. We search farther for the paradise of the wild. But the wild is here: nature is in our own backyards, our vacant lots, our office parks. We can restore and steward these spaces, untended and maligned though they may currently be. Those weedy plants are right here, in situ, tapping us on the shoulder, poking at our ankles, waiting for us to find them, to know them, and to forage them.

Out of 6,000 total plants in the wild flora of the area, I fraternize with about 300, of which maybe 100 are edible. According to the 2020 Kew Gardens report *State of the World's Plants and Fungi*, there are at least 7,039 edible plant species in the world, but only 417 are considered food crops. With a large percentage of the "agricultural" land considered "degraded," there is an urgent need to find new sources of food plants that are resilient and nutritious. Are we prepared for the next blight, pest, weather change? Am I clinging to a world that has already gone?

The thousands of underutilized and neglected plant species, known as orphan crops, are the lifeline to millions of people on Earth tormented by unprecedented climate change, pervasive food and nutrition insecurity and economic development... Harnessing this basket of untapped resources for making food and production systems more diverse and resilient to change, should be our moral duty to current and future generations. KEW GARDENS, *STATE OF THE WORLD'S PLANTS AND FUNGI*

Let's give some of these plants a second chance. Let's reimagine the way we view the plants around us and make them into something delicious, wanted, and respected. We don't need to create a garden that mimics nature, because nature is here.

As for me, I have reached a sort of equilibrium where I live. Each place spins on a slightly different axis of seasons, plants, and habitats. You can't import them back with you, though you may try a plant or two. I return to my garden, but I also travel within a several-hour radius and beyond; there are communities of foragers, plant people, naturalists who share their own spots. Within each season I travel from place to place, a nomadic habit for families, tribes, people for thousands of years. Seeking cooling in the summer, warmth in the cooler months this didn't mean that the grounds were not tended because someone didn't live on premises for twelve months. The streambeds could be managed when present and then left to rest until the next year. I start February often about three hours south and then move to my place from May on. In summer I branch up and down, especially near the sea breezes. Autumn means back into the woods for fruit and mushrooms. In the West, my forager friends spend winters and spring in the woods for mushrooms, summer up north and to the coast for berry picking. We are nomads and discoverers; not a week goes by without some kind of "adventure." We also return to the same places time and again—some not seen since last year—refreshed and also missing them. No matter where I am heading, at the end of the day, I still carry in my mind's eye last season's images, driving down county roads where I live: the hills, the spreading sky and the shifting light among the clouds. I try to drink it in as much as I can, knowing it will shift soon enough.

WILD FARMING

A decade ago I crossed over the bridge from forage to garden to farm. I call it a wild farm. Instead of trying to change the land to farm a crop that doesn't naturally grow in that place, why not change the definition of an acceptable "crop" to farm, and restore that plant that would have, should have, grown there wild?

Of course I started with the "low-hanging fruit": in this case, sumac. I still remember the look on Daniel Boulud's face when Eddy gave him the paper bag with the *je ne sais quoi* inside. Surprises bring out his inner curiosity. But, of course, he had already known the Mediterranean sumac for years and found the American sumac was superior in complexity, tart but not sour, fruity and with nutty notes. And so healthy. Once I figured out how to work with it, I needed more.

"Everyone" told me, "oh yeah, sumac, that's everywhere." It's funny how once you start looking for something that is "extremely common," it seems to have disappeared from so many places, except for inaccessible places like off the highway—and even then, I noticed, sadly, that the road department is target spraying staghorn sumac off the I-95 in Pennsylvania. I was having to go farther and farther afield to collect the fruit in the fall. I would always ask permission, and people were only too

happy as they considered it a nuisance or, worse, poison sumac (it's not the same! See the section on poisonous plants, page 70).

The farm hedgerows were thorny and shrubby, or vanished altogether. On closer inspection I noticed a couple things that were slamming the sumac:

- **Removal.** Sumac likes to grow out in a suckering fashion. After a few years, the initial leader will die back and the suckers shoot up. So, farmers would mow them down or mow around the edges year after year so the sumac started to get weaker.

- **Strangling and competition** from grapevines, honeysuckle vines, and invasives.

- **Deer.** The white-tailed deer love the fresh shoots of sumac leaves and will eat an entire grove down in a couple hours. Also, the bucks like to rub against the bark.

I decided I wanted to restore an area of sumac where there normally would have been one, but it was now lost between a patchwork of lawn meeting hayfield. It was only a few acres, but it sat in a key corridor joining two preserved forests, a bucolic south-facing slope looking down over rolling hills. The farmer wanted me to "do something" with the slope as it was annoying for him to keep mowing it and it was too steep to suit most crops.

I knew it would take more than just seeing what is there. Because it had been hayed and farmed for so long, some intervention was required other than just letting hay grass grow long. And also it was "farmland," so it had to be "farmed" with a "crop." But the list of crops never had wild plants. I didn't want to choose crops that never belonged to the land and then try to amend the land to accommodate and prop up the crop. Instead, it took only a trick of the mind to say, let's keep the land and change our contrived definition of a crop. Why can't a weed be a crop?

Thus started the I Am a Weed Farm. The crops would be plants that grew there or closely replicated what would be there. There were no structures for irrigation, large-scale machinery, greenhouses, cover fabrics, tilling. A bunch of us worked with a native plant nursery and planted sumac trees in different growth stages: tree, bare-root, plugs, and seed. No mulch, no fertilizer, no irrigation.

Was this a garden? Agriculture? Horticulture? People asked me, isn't a "wild farm" an oxymoron? No, it's the way of the Middle Ground. We took some data points to compare seeds, plugs, bare-root plants, and young trees. What plants like to be around sumac? No one seemed to have an answer. So we watched and waited. In a year we had our answer: the community of plants includes wild hornbeam, gray dogwood, silky dogwood, narrow-leafed mountain mint, common milkweed. We did have to manage the plot to keep back the poison ivy and keep invasive Japanese honeysuckle vine at bay.

Our definitions of "rotating" and "diverse" crops and gardens cannot mimic nature, where one square meter of meadow might contain forty-five different plants, rotating every two to four weeks instead of once or twice a year. Just throw off the badges, the titles, the social attainments, the preoccupations and daily to-do lists. Throw off the idea of making something grand and awesome; strip the mind naked and start again, in a true garden.

Epilogue

"Just don't let the noise of others' opinions drown out your own inner voice . . . .
Stay hungry. Stay foolish."

—STEVE JOBS

Running forward into an unknown future. If you had asked me about my vision for a plan, the mission, the business, I would have told you my focus was on: the state of wild plants in the world, stretching past the borders of my town and disrupting the definition of crops. But now, I'm not so sure. These things are still the foundations for where I think we need to go. But I'm no longer sure how to get there, if I ever was. The pandemic has thrown the lid off our lives and assumptions; we can no longer blithely trust that things are just going to turn out all right. Opportunistic before, my small team now works on a weekly pivot, not looking too far ahead on an unknown path. We never did know the path, it's just that now we are starkly aware that we do not know the way.

During the COVID lockdown we were not permitted to go anywhere, and I was confined to the area right around my house. I could go only short distances, displaying a special "Essential Food Product Work Being Done" certificate. But even as things eased, they didn't cease, and I spent more time outdoors in the garden. I was alone a lot of the time, an empty nester, my husband volunteering for rescue squad duty, which at times was all-consuming. For lack of company, I noticed I would talk to myself. When reading a book, if I discovered some new connection (like the chrysanthemums or the Middle Ground), I would shout out loud, laughing and whooping. It didn't matter, because no one could hear me. I could fall off my chair excitedly. I could mutter to myself. And I started talking in the garden...to a turtle, a bird, a praying mantis, a dragonfly on my shoulder. And to plants. I was left to my own ways, without judgment. Sometimes not even using words, just melodic sounds; half-formed words that lilt up and down, like a tune. I make these same noises sometimes when I "speak" to young children or babies, sidling alongside them, not looking directly into their face as if I expect something from them. Or to the autistic ladies who come over once a week to press labels and wander in the field. And I have come to communicate intuitively with my father, my once brilliant scientist father, now unable to speak in whole sentences. We communicate in this other way and I know it pleases him as I see the grin spread across his face.

These last few years I have changed as well. I begin to wake at dawn, or sometimes the hour before the sun rises, when sounds are hushed and shapes are dim. But my mind is clear. I smile secretly because today there is nothing scheduled. The day extends, boundless, before me, like the curtain rising on a grand play. I do not know the actors, but I have faith that there are parts to be played.

"Where are you off to now?" My husband calls to me from the den as I bang up the stairs to get the special clippers I forgot. I mutter something as I bang down the stairs, but it doesn't really matter—I could say the bog, and I end up in the forest, or the preserve; I could say the meadow and I end up in the vegetable beds. I'm going off to dance with nature. As the screen door slams behind me, I can hear his fading triumphant retort: "You're becoming just like your mother!"

Waking Up to the World
The fog of sleep lifts
And this shining world
Comes back into view:
Dew in the meadow,
Sunlight on the leaves,
Cherry blossoms in bloom,
A blue jewel of sky.

What else have we
Been sleeping through?

—MATTHEW FOLEY, 2018

Acknowledgments

This writing began at a time when we were surrounded by illness and death, a pandemic, the usual rhythms broken, turning for solace to the nature close by, more time to observe and reflect. It is only a snapshot in time and place, of where I came from, what I was doing, and where I might be going, reflecting the collective experiences and tales of mentors, advisors, experts, colleagues and journey mates, parents, children, and grandparents. For in the face of great change in the natural world, the best we can do is form a community of sorts, and I am deeply grateful for the counsel, camaraderie, and goodwill of this band of "homies" who are foragers, scientists, teachers, gardeners, land stewards, chefs, farmers, naturalists, and nature lovers.

I would particularly like to thank: Lena Struwe and Alex McAlvay for their enthusiastic and patient discussions of curious plant-related botanical and ethnobotanical questions. And to Ian Caton, Troy Ettel, Dr. Gerould Wilhelm, Karl Anderson, and Michael Van Clef for their decades of plant wisdom.

To the merry team of Skye King and Derek Carty, with their passion for the outdoors and the flora and fungi. To Max Reed for his storytelling and resourcefulness, to Jade Greene, to Mayfield Williams, Doug Hara, and in absentia yet always present: Larry Rossi and Norma Chow Matsuoka.

To Jenny Wapner, Sharon Bowers, and Carolyn Insley for believing in my belief even though it was not yet out in the world, and to Ngoc, Bobbi, my dear spouse Wil, and Toni Tajima for taking a Word document and bringing it alive.

Thank you.

Index

A

Ailanthus altissima. See tree of
    heaven
air, 21
ajuga, in leis, 218–19
Allium spp., 88–89
Amanita family, 74
American germander (*Teucrium
    canadense*), 124, 175
annuals, 148
Anthriscus sylvestris. See cow parsnip
apples
    about, 198
    Feral Apple Spread, 199
Aralia elata. See Japanese angelica
    tree
aromatics, 220
arrangements, wild plants in, 211–12,
    214–15
Artemisia vulgaris. See mugwort

B

bamboo, 153
basil
    in arrangements, 212
    Lemon Basil and Wild Lemon
        Balm Pesto, 170–71

varieties of, 170
bee balm (*Monarda didyma*), 99, 175
beech (*Fagus grandifolia*), 25–26
Bernstein, Scott, 146
berries
    freezing, 189
    identifying, 74
    Sour Cherry and Wild Berry
        Jam, 191
Berry, Wendell, 96
biannuals, 148
Bidens, 175
blueberries, freezing, 189
Boulud, Daniel, 93, 228
Brassicaceae, 84–85
broccoli rabe, wild (*Brassica rapa*),
    84–85
burning, 71

C

cages, 28–29
Camellia sinensis. See tea
Cardamine hirsuta. See upland cress
cedar, 75
ceremonies, 220
chaga (*Inonotus obliquus*), 74
change, 107–9

Chenopodium spp. *See* lambsquarters
cherries
    freezing, 189
    Sour Cherry and Wild Berry
        Jam, 191
chestnuts, 108–9
chicken of the woods (*Laetiporus
    sulphureus*), 74
chicken wire
    about, 28
    cages, 28–29
    fences, 128, 130
    flower frog, 216–17
    standard roll of, 28
    trellis, 132–35
    uses for, 27
chickweed (*Stellaria media*), 87, 177
chives, wild (*Allium* spp.), 88–89
chrysanthemums, 152, 170, 208,
    218, 230
Cicuta virosa. See water hemlock
citrus leaves, cooking with, 179
clammy goosefoot (*Dysphania
    pumilia*)
    about, 78–79
    Clammy Goosefoot Forager's
        Salad Dressing, 79

"climax" forest, 104
Cohen, Amanda, 79
compost
  about, 117–18
  bin center, 118, 120–21
  piles, 118
Comptonia peregrina. See sweet fern
Conium maculatum. See poison
  hemlock
construction sites, rescuing plants
  form, 181–82
cow parsnip (*Anthriscus sylvestris*),
  71, 125
crates, 125
creeping Jenny (*Lysimachia
  rummularia*), 172
cultivar names, 69
cut and come again, 177
cuttings, 169–70, 172

D

dandelion (*Taraxacum officinale*)
  about, 81–82
  blooming, 21
  leaf study, 66
  life cycle of, 148
Daucus carota. See Queen
  Anne's lace
death, 105–6
decapitation method, 152
deer
  about, 156
  fence, 128, 156–59
  sumac and, 228
dormancy, 105–6
drinks
  Fig Leaf Gimlet, 194–95
  Spruce Tip Mocktail, 192–93
driveway poles, 27
drying, 200
Dysphania pumilia. See clammy
  goosefoot

E

edge
  definition of, 16
  making, with wild wood, 34
edging
  open-lashed, 38, 40–41
  woven wattle, 36–37
evening primrose (*Oenothera
  biennis*), 124
evergreens
  identifying, 74
  needles, drying, 200

F

Fagus grandifolia. See beech
Fallopia japonica. See Japanese
  knotweed
farming, wild, 228–29
fences, 128, 130
fennel, wild (*Foeniculum vulgare*),
  124, 148
Feral Apple Spread, 199
ferments, 197
fertilizer, 117
field rhythms, 99–100
fig leaves
  about, 194
  Fig Leaf Gimlet, 194–95
  Fig Leaf Syrup, 194–95
firestarters, juniper, 223
floriography, 220
flower frogs
  chicken wire, 216–17
  kenzan, 214
Foeniculum vulgare. See fennel, wild
Foley, Matthew, 231
foraging, 15–16, 74–76
frame trellis, 132–35
Francis, Pope, 143
freezing, 189–90
frost line, 60
fruits
  drying, 200
  freezing, 189
  See also individual fruits

G

Galinsoga (*G. parviflora, G.
  quadriradiata*), 90–91, 146, 175
Galium aparine. See sticky willy
gardening
  field rhythms and, 99–100
  with intention, 11
  See also raised beds; wild
  gardens
garlic, wild. *See* chives, wild
garlic pennycress (*Thlaspi alliaceum,
  T. arvense*)., 149, 150
gates
  attaching, to a post, 60–61
  making, 56, 58–59
giant hogweed (*Heracleum
  mantegazzianum*), 71
gin
  Fig Leaf Gimlet, 194–95
goldmoss (*Sedum acre*), 172
grapes, 136
grasses, 101
Green, Connie, 196
greens
  drying, 200
  freezing, 189, 190
grow lights, 180
Gynura crepioiedes. See longevity
  spinach
G. procumbens. See longevity
  spinach

H

Hamamelis virginiana. See witch
  hazel
harvest protocols, wild, 188
Heracleum mantegazzianum. See
  giant hogweed
herbicides, 151
herbs, drying, 200
honeysuckle. *See* Japanese
  honeysuckle
Huberman, Andrew, 20

I

identification tips, 73–76
ikebana, 27, 211, 212, 217
Inonotus obliquus. See chaga
invasive plants, 150–53
itching, 70–71

J

Jam, Sour Cherry and Wild Berry, 191
Japanese angelica tree (*Aralia elata*), 71, 152
Japanese honeysuckle (*Lonicera japonica*)
    Honeysuckle Tea, 206
    as invasive plant, 153
    as twining vine, 136
Japanese knotweed (*Reynoutria japonica, Fallopia japonica*)
    harvesting, 154
    as invasive plant, 150
    Japanese Knotweed Pickle and Soda, 155
Jobs, Steve, 230
Juncus effusus. See rush, common
juniper (*Juniperus* spp.)
    about, 95
    berries, drying, 200
    firestarters, 223

K

kenzan, 214
Kuester, Nate, 155

L

labels, 42–43
Laetiporus sulphureus. See chicken of the woods
lambsquarters (*Chenopodium* spp.), 18, 76–78
Laportea canadensis. See wood nettle
lavender bergamot (*Monarda fistulosa*), 176

layering, horizontal and vertical, 51
leis, wildflower, 218–19
Lemon Basil and Wild Lemon Balm Pesto, 170–71
Leroux, Eddy, 93, 153, 228
Let Standing method, 17–18, 163
light
    from grow lights, 180
    natural, 20–21
Liljengren, Heather, 166
limes
    Fig Leaf Gimlet, 194–95
    Lime Leaf, Galangal, and Lemongrass Meatballs, 179
    Spruce Tip Mocktail, 192–93
longevity spinach (*Gynura crepioiedes, G. procumbens*), 177, 178
Lonicera japonica. See Japanese honeysuckle
Lysimachia rummularia. See creeping Jenny

M

mast years, 107
Matricaria discoidea. See pineapple weed
mayapple, 25
meadows
    doctoring, 102–3
    pocket, 176
Meatballs, Lime Leaf, Galangal, and Lemongrass, 179
Middle Ground, wild gardens of the, 17–18
Mishima, Yukio, 44
Mitchell, Joni, 8
Monarda didyma. See bee balm
M. fistulosa. See lavender bergamot
monastery gardens, 220
mountain mint (*Pycnanthemum muticum, P. tenufolium*), 176
mugwort (*Artemisia vulgaris*), 151–52
Mulberry Shrub, 196

mulch, 117
mushrooms
    drying, 200
    identifying, 74
mustards, 84–85
myoga ginger (*Zingiber mioga*), 42

N

nageire, 214
Natufians, 17, 220
nodes, 149
nuts, harvesting, 107–9

O

Oenothera biennis. See evening primrose
open-lashed edging, 38, 40–41
Origanum syriacum. See za'atar
Oxalis oregana. See western wood sorrel
O. stricta. See wood sorrel

P

parsnip, wild (*Pastinaca sativa*), 71
passionflower (*Passiflora incarnata*)
    genetic diversity of, 163
    tea, 211
    as tendril vine, 136
Pastinaca sativa. See parsnip, wild
patches, enclosing wild(ish), 30, 32–33
paths
    labels for, 42–43
    making, 54
    value of, 52
pawpaws, freezing, 189
peas, 136
perennials, 148
Pesto, Lemon Basil and Wild Lemon Balm, 170–71
Phlox paniculata, 69
phytophotodermatitis, 71
pineapple weed (*Matricaria discoidea*), 211

plants
    to avoid, 70–72
    bringing indoors, 177
    buying, 173
    growth habits of, 149
    identification tips for, 73–76
    invasive, 150–53
    knowing, 65
    labels for, 42–43
    life cycles of, 148
    mixing, in beds, 123–24
    naming, 68–69
    poisonous, 72
    rescuing, 181–82
    seasons of, 101
    tending, 143
    transplanting, 173–75
    See also individual plants
plugs, 123
poison hemlock (*Conium maculatum*), 72
poison ivy (*Toxicodendron* spp.), 70
poison oak (*Toxicodendron diversilobum; T. pubescens*), 70–71
poisonous plants, 72
poison sumac (*Toxicodendron vernix*), 70
Pollan, Michael, 77
pork
    Lime Leaf, Galangal, and Lemongrass Meatballs, 179
Portulaca oleracea. See purslane
prickles, 71
prickly pear cactus, trichomes on, 72
purslane (*Portulaca oleracea*), 80–81
Pycnanthemum muticum. See mountain mint
P. tenufolium. See mountain mint

Q
Queen Anne's lace (*Daucus carota*), 71, 72, 148

R
rabbits, 125, 128
raised beds
    annexes for, 131
    characteristics of, 113
    fences and other protection for, 125, 128, 130
    filling, 117–18
    kits for, 113
    making and placing, 116
    mixing plants in, 123–24
    as test beds, 113, 124
ramp, wild (*Allium tricoccum*), 89
Reynoutria japonica. See Japanese knotweed
rhizomes
    about, 149
    growing plants from, 172
    of invasive plants, 151–52
Rhoads, Anne Fowler, 73
Rhus typhina. See sumac
roadsides, rescuing plants form, 181–82
rocks, 27
Rumex acetosella. See sheep sorrel
rush, common (*Juncus effusus*), 21

S
Salad Dressing, Clammy Goosefoot Forager's, 79
Sanmi, Sasaki, 151–52
seasons, 101
Sedum acre. See goldmoss
seeds
    about, 163
    collecting, 165–67
    sowing, 168–69
    storing, 168
sheep sorrel (*Rumex acetosella*), 86
shrubs
    about, 196
    Mulberry Shrub, 196
signs, 42–43

Sinclair, David, 106
smudge sticks, 222
soil
    amendments, 117
    local, 117
    in wild gardens, 21
solarization, 151, 152
Solidago patula. See swamp goldenrod
spines, 71–72
spots, marking, 27
Spread, Feral Apple, 199
spruce
    identifying, 75
    Spruce Tip Mocktail, 192–93
    Spruce Tip Syrup, 192
Stellaria media. See chickweed
sticky willy (*Galium aparine*), 72
stinging nettle (*Urtica dioica*)
    about, 91–92
    tea, 211
    trichomes on, 72
stone, 27
Struwe, Lena, 78, 146
succession, 104
suckers, 149
sumac (*Rhus typhina*)
    about, 93–94
    growth habits of, 149
    sowing seeds of, 168
    tea, 211
    wild farming, 228–29
swamp goldenrod (*Solidago patula*), 26
sweet fern (*Comptonia peregrina*), 211
syrups
    about, 192
    fermented, 197
    Fig Leaf Syrup, 194–95
    Spruce Tip Syrup, 192

T

Tallamy, Douglas W., 69
Taraxacum officinale. See dandelion
tea
    culture of, 205–6
    Honeysuckle Tea, 206
    making, 206
    passionflower, 211
    pineapple weed, 211
    stinging nettle, 211
    sumac, 211
    sweet fern, 211
Teucrium canadense. See American
    germander
Thlaspi alliaceum. See garlic
    pennycress
T. arvense. See garlic pennycress
thorns, 71
tinctures, 197
Toxicodendron, 70–71
transplanting, 173–75
tree of heaven (*Ailanthus altissima*),
    93
trellis, 132–35
trench planting, 175
trichomes, 72

U

Umbelliferae, 71, 148
upland cress (*Cardamine hirsuta*),
    163, 165, 177
Urtica dioica. See stinging nettle
Uva, Richard, 73

V

vacant lots, rescuing plants form,
    181–82
vernal ponds, 25
views, 47–48
vines
    support for, 136, 138–39
    tendril, 136
    twining, 136
violets (*Viola* spp.), 181

W

wandering, 52
water
    managing wild, 49
    in wild gardens, 21
water hemlock (*Cicuta virosa*), 72
wattle edging, woven, 36–37
waves, 107
weeding, 143, 145–46
western wood sorrel (*Oxalis
    oregana*), 86
white, symbolism of, 211
wild farming, 228–29
wild gardens
    characteristics of, 15, 19–20, 220
    design elements of, 20–21
    of the Middle Ground, 17–18
    views of, 47–48

wild wood
    gates, 56, 58–59
    making an edge with, 34
Wilhelm, Gerould, 68, 163
wisteria, 136
witch hazel (*Hamamelis virginiana*),
    26
wood, drying, 200
woodchucks, 128
wood nettle (*Laportea canadensis*),
    92
wood sorrel (*Oxalis stricta*), 86

X

Xenohormesis Hypothesis, 106

Y

yarrow, 32, 34, 48, 172, 175
yew, 75

Z

za'atar (*Origanum syriacum*), 48, 170,
    177
Zheng Ban-Qiao, 208
Zingiber mioga. See myoga ginger

54397742R00018